How to Use This Book

Look for these special features in this book:

SIDEBARS, **CHARTS**, **GRAPHS**, and original **MAPS** expand your understanding of what's being discussed—and also make useful sources for classroom reports.

FAQs answer common **F**requently **A**sked **Q**uestions about people, places, and things.

WOW FACTORS offer "Who knew?" facts to keep you thinking.

TRAVEL GUIDE gives you tips on exploring the state—either in person or right from your chair!

PROJECT ROOM provides fun ideas for school assignments and incredible research projects. Plus, there's a guide to primary sources—what they are and how to cite them.

Please note: All statistics are as up-to-date as possible at the time of publication.

Consultant: Michael B. Ballard, Coordinator, Congressional and Political Research Center and University Archivist, Mississippi State University; William Loren Katz; Maurice A. Meylan, Professor of Geology, University of Southern Mississippi

Book production by The Design Lab

Library of Congress Cataloging-in-Publication Data
Dell, Pamela.
 Mississippi / by Pamela Dell.
    p. cm.—(America the beautiful. Third series)
Includes bibliographical references and index.
ISBN-13: 978-0-531-18563-6
ISBN-10: 0-531-18563-X
1. Mississippi—Juvenile literature. I. Title.
F341.3.D45 2008
976.2—dc22   2006101965

1 2 3 4 5 6 7 8 9 10 R 17 16 15 14 13 12 11 10 09 08

AMERICA ★ THE ★ BEAUTIFUL

Mississippi

BY PAMELA DELL

Third Series

Children's Press®
An Imprint of Scholastic Inc.
New York ★ Toronto ★ London ★ Auckland ★ Sydney
Mexico City ★ New Delhi ★ Hong Kong
Danbury, Connecticut

CONTENTS

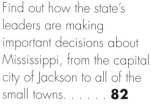

TENNESSEE

N
W E
S

0   40
Miles

Mississippi

Woodall
Mountain

Tennessee

Delta Blues
Museum

TUPELO

Tombigbee
National
Forest

Elvis Presley
Birthplace

CLARKSDALE

ARKANSAS

Natchez Trace Parkway

Tombigbee

COLUMBUS

GREENVILLE

Delta region

MISSISSIPPI

ALABAMA

Birthplace of
the Frog
Museum

Yazoo

Petrified forest

'Voices of the Civil
Rights Movement Bus Tour'

LOUISIANA

The Grand Village
of the Natchez

JACKSON

Bienville
National
Forest

MERIDIAN

Jackson State
Capitol

Mississippi
River

NATCHEZ

Pearl

HATTIESBURG

Leaf

Pascagoula River,
the "singing" river

Mississippi Sandhill Crane
National Wildlife Refuge

John C. Stennis
Space Center

Pascagoula

Friendship Oak

GULFPORT   BILOXI

PASCAGOULA

QUICK FACTS

State capital: Jackson
Largest city: Jackson
Total area: 48,430 square miles
(125,434 sq km)
Highest point: Woodall Mountain,
806 feet (246 m)
Lowest point: Sea level at the
Gulf Coast

GULF OF MEXICO

Welcome to Mississippi!

HOW DID MISSISSIPPI GET ITS NAME?

Long before the United States was on any map, the Native people of North America had given different names to a mighty river. It flows from its source in Lake Itasca in present-day Minnesota to the Gulf of Mexico. To the Algonquins, the river was known as the *messipi*, or "big river." The Ojibwas, or Chippewas, called it the *misi-ziibi*, or "great river." And in the language of the Choctaws, the largest Native American nation in the Mississippi region, the river was known as *misha sipokni*, translated variously as "older than time," "beyond age," and "father of waters."

Spanish and French explorers interpreted the Indian names as "Mississippi." Eventually, this region would earn statehood under the same name.

8

READ ABOUT

This coastal swamp in Mississippi is an example of the state's diverse landscape.

CHAPTER ONE

LAND

★

THROUGHOUT MISSISSIPPI'S 48,430 SQUARE MILES (125,434 SQUARE KILOMETERS), THE SWEET FRAGRANCES OF HONEYSUCKLE AND MAGNOLIA ARE IN THE AIR. The Gulf of Mexico laps at white sandy beaches along the southern coast. Mississippi's low land slopes gently from the state's northern border, eventually reaching sea level at the Gulf of Mexico. Its highest point is at Woodall Mountain, just 806 feet (246 meters), and its lowest point is at sea level on the Gulf. But the Magnolia State is a place filled with rich landscapes, from the steep bluffs to coastal sands.

LAND LAND LAND LAND LAND

This is a present-day image of the Gulf of Mexico off the Mississippi and Alabama coasts.

THE FORMATION OF MISSISSIPPI

Oceans have covered the land that is now Mississippi many times over the course of millions of years. The shells of sea creatures were left behind and formed limestone, which helped plant life grow in the sun. The dead bodies of these creatures formed oil and gas deposits. The soil grew rich with sandstone, clay, lignite, and other materials that are now among the state's natural resources.

When the last ice age ended about 10,000 years ago, **glaciers** that covered much of the continent melted, leaving a huge amount of water. At one point, an enormous bay extended from the Gulf of Mexico all the way to Minnesota! As this bay shrank, the water formed the

Mississippi River, from the northern part of the present-day United States to the Gulf. Silt and sand deposits at the mouth of the river created fertile land at its southern end. Over the ages, vegetation covered this area and created the land we now know as Mississippi.

Today, you will see shimmering flatlands in the Delta region. Its sun-baked cotton, soy, and rice fields stretch away from the slowly winding Mississippi River. And you'll travel through wild hill country in the cool shade of the state's vast stretches of pine forest.

Mississippi's southern coast curves around the Gulf of Mexico, and its southwestern border runs along the state of Louisiana. The mighty Mississippi River forms a natural border between the two states. Mississippi shares its eastern border with Alabama. Tennessee lies directly to the north, and Arkansas is to the northwest.

Mississippi Geo-Facts

Along with the state's geographical highlights, this chart ranks Mississippi's land, water, and total area compared to all other states.

Total area; rank . . . . 48,430 square miles (125,434 sq km); 32nd
    Land; rank . . . . 46,907 square miles (121,489 sq km); 31st
    Water; rank . . . . 1,523 square miles (3,945 sq km); 24th
    Inland water; rank . . . . 785 square miles (2,033 sq km); 27th
    Coastal water; rank . . . . 590 square miles (1,528 sq km); 10th
    Territorial water; rank . . . . 148 square miles (383 sq km); 19th
Geographic center . . . . Leake County, 9 miles (14 km) northwest of Carthage
Latitude . . . . 30° 13′ N to 35° N
Longitude . . . . 88° 7′ W to 91° 41′ W
Highest point . . . . Woodall Mountain, 806 feet (246 m)
Lowest point . . . . Sea level at the Gulf Coast
Largest city . . . . Jackson
Longest river . . . . Mississippi River

Source: U.S. Census Bureau

Mississippi is the 32nd-largest state in the nation. Rhode Island could fit inside Mississippi more than 31 times!

Mississippi's Topography

Use the color-coded elevation chart to see on the map Mississippi's high points (orange) and low points (green to dark green). Elevation is measured as the distance above or below sea level.

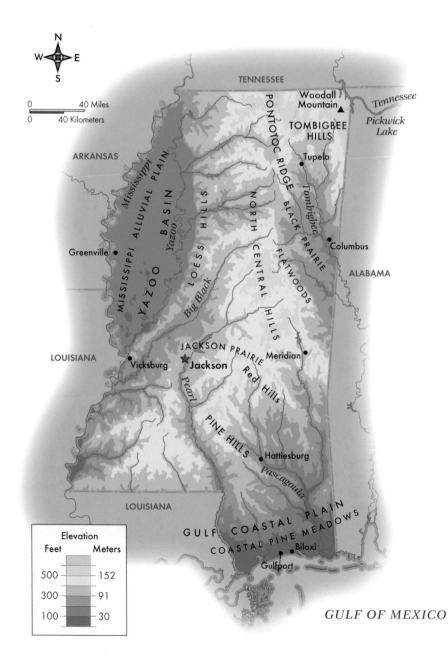

GULF OF MEXICO

Elevation	
Feet	Meters
500	152
300	91
100	30

LAND REGIONS

Mississippi lies almost completely in the East Gulf Coastal Plain. This area stretches from the Tennessee border in the north straight down to the Gulf Coast. It is part of the Atlantic and Gulf Coastal Plain that reaches from New England all the way to eastern Mexico. Within the state, there are 10 geographic regions: the Tombigbee Hills, the Black Prairie, the Pontotoc Ridge, the Flatwoods, the North Central Hills, the Loess Hills, the Mississippi **Alluvial** Plain, the Jackson Prairie, the Pine Hills, and the Coastal Pine Meadows.

Tombigbee Hills, Black Prairie, and Pontotoc Ridge

Also called the Tennessee River Hills, the Tombigbee Hills region is the innermost part of the East Gulf Coastal Plain. It's an area of rugged hills that lies in the northeastern part of the state. The Tombigbee Hills have an average elevation of 650 feet (200 m). The region is drained by the Tombigbee and Tennessee rivers.

The Black Prairie is a narrow belt of land also in the northeastern part of Mississippi. It is a fairly flat area with fewer trees and an average width of only 20 to 25 miles (32 to 40 km). The name comes from the dark color of its rich soil, which is excellent for growing cotton, hay, and corn.

The Pontotoc Ridge serves as a divide between the Mississippi River basin to the west and the Tennessee and Tombigbee basins to the east. It is a hilly region with sand that has weathered to a reddish color.

Flatwoods, North Central Hills, and Loess Hills

The width of this region varies from 6 to 12 miles (10 to 19 km). The area is flat and lies between the Pontotoc Ridge and the North Central Hills.

WORD TO KNOW

alluvial *sand, silt, clay, and gravel that are deposited by running water*

Ranging from 400 to 600 feet (100 to 200 m) above sea level, the North Central Hills region is the most extensive upland in the state. It is part of the Red Hills area, a larger region that continues into south-central Alabama.

The Loess Hills region extends along the western part of the state. It gets its name from the deposits of loess found there. Loess is a fertile kind of silt that is a light orange-yellow color. It helps form the steep slopes of the area.

The Mississippi Alluvial Plain

Forming the western margin of the state, this region is a **floodplain** formed by continual flooding of the Mississippi River. As the water spills over the land, it leaves rich alluvial deposits, which results in some of the richest soil in the United States. This hot, sunbaked region is farm country, which produces rice, soybeans, and cotton.

The land is accented by slight elevations that act as natural **levees**. Mississippians sometimes call this area the Yazoo Basin or the Delta.

WORDS TO KNOW

floodplain *land next to a river or stream that experiences periodic flooding*

levees *human-made embankments used to prevent flooding*

Rice fields stretch for miles in some regions of the state.

This region contains the state's fascinating Petrified Forest and many of Mississippi's oxbow lakes. These are U-shaped bodies of water that were at one time curving sections of the Mississippi River. As the river changed its course over the years, it cut away from some of these curves, isolating them and turning them into the oxbow lakes.

Jackson Prairie, Pine Hills, and Coastal Pine Meadows

Fairly flat, the Jackson Prairie lies in a narrow belt extending from Clarke to Madison counties in the central part of the state. Some parts of the area are made of weathered clay, while others consist of limestone. These materials help support the cement industry in the state.

The Pine Hills region is high and rolling, with most of the area between 300 and 500 feet (90 and 150 m) above sea level. At one time, it was known as the Longleaf Pine Belt, because of the longleaf pines that were common there. The region is in the southern part of the state, bordering part of Louisiana as well as the Coastal Pine Meadows.

Extending inland 15 to 20 miles (25 to 30 km), the Coastal Pine Meadows area is fairly flat and made of fine sand. It forms the southernmost strip of Mississippi.

CLIMATE

When you think about Mississippi's climate, two words may come to mind: hot and humid! It's a land of long, hot summers and short, mild winters. Midsummer temperatures in the state average around 81 degrees Fahrenheit (27 degrees Celsius), but occasionally reach the high 90s (36–37°C). Breezes from the Gulf of Mexico

SEE IT HERE!

MISSISSIPPI PETRIFIED FOREST

This national natural landmark in Flora features strange-looking fallen timbers that have turned to stone! About 36 million years ago, downed trees clogged a waterway. The river changed its course and continued on its way, leaving the trees behind. Over time, the unused channels where the trees lay filled up with mud, sand, and other debris, which covered the trees. Minerals filled the spaces between the trees' woody tissue, gradually petrifying them into gigantic stone logs. Erosion uncovered Mississippi's petrified trees in the mid-1800s. It is the only petrified forest east of the Mississippi River.

One particular log in the Mississippi Petrified Forest is less than 6 feet long (1.8 m) but weighs 1,685 pounds (764 kilograms)!

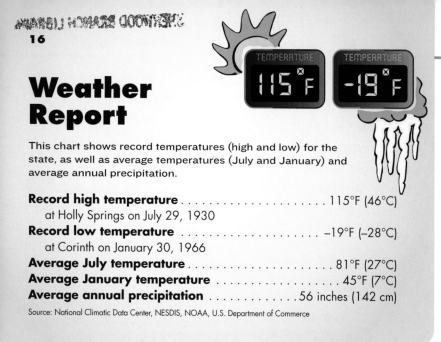

Weather Report

This chart shows record temperatures (high and low) for the state, as well as average temperatures (July and January) and average annual precipitation.

Record high temperature . . . . 115°F (46°C)
at Holly Springs on July 29, 1930
Record low temperature . . . . –19°F (–28°C)
at Corinth on January 30, 1966
Average July temperature . . . . 81°F (27°C)
Average January temperature . . . . 45°F (7°C)
Average annual precipitation . . . . .56 inches (142 cm)

Source: National Climatic Data Center, NESDIS, NOAA, U.S. Department of Commerce

help cool things down, so it's rare for the mercury to soar past 100°F (38°C).

By January, Mississippi's average temperature is 45°F (7°C). On the coast, winter months are often frost-free, but central and northern Mississippi may see snow and ice, which can occasionally cause millions of dollars in damages.

Mississippi is a fairly wet place, mostly owing to rain. In the coastal region, the precipitation averages about 65 inches (165 centimeters) a year. In the drier northwestern part of the state, the annual precipitation average is about 50 inches (127 cm). Thunderstorms roll in frequently, particularly in the spring and late summer. Sometimes these storms develop into tornadoes, which begin on land, or hurricanes, which start over water. Hurricane season begins about midsummer and can last into October. Tornado season is usually from spring through the end of summer.

DEADLY DISASTER

In August 2005, the Gulf Coast was battered by Hurricane Katrina, one of the most devastating storms in U.S. history. It ripped along the Louisiana, Alabama, and Mississippi coastlines, bringing violent winds and flooding that caused billions of dollars in damage and took almost 2,000 lives throughout the Gulf region.

Katrina moved into Mississippi with winds of more than 120 miles (193 km) per hour, causing tremendous

Residents of Biloxi search through debris for their belongings after Hurricane Katrina destroyed their neighborhood.

destruction in many cities along the coast. The hurricane destroyed two major bridges and left 238 people dead and nearly 70 missing. It also set off 11 tornadoes across inland Mississippi. Officials estimated that within a half mile (800 m) of the coast, only 10 percent of the structures remained standing once Katrina had passed through.

Since the storm, the Mississippi, Alabama, and Louisiana coastal regions have begun to rebound. Volunteers are rebuilding homes, businesses, and entire communities. Slowly but surely, they are restoring the region to its original beauty.

Spanish moss, which hangs from these trees, is a gray plant that's actually related to the pineapple.

WORD TO KNOW

bayous *streams that run slowly through swamps and lead to or from a river*

The 500-year-old Friendship Oak in Long Beach, Mississippi, stands 50 feet (15 m) tall and has a trunk that's 17 feet (5 m) around. The tree's spreading foliage provides 16,000 square feet (5,000 sq m) of shelter!

PLANT LIFE

Talk about trees! More than 50 percent of the state of Mississippi is forestland. Many species of fragrant pines grow here, as do sweet gum, ash, cottonwood, oak, hickory, elm, tupelo, and pecan trees. Bald cypress trees are common in Mississippi's **bayous** and swamps, where they grow right out of the water. Spanish moss hangs from many of these trees, giving them a uniquely strange and southern look.

The magnolia tree is the official state tree, and it provides beautiful, fragrant white blossoms that sweeten the Mississippi air. The magnolia also has the honor of being the state flower. In the springtime, Mississippi is a marvel of natural color! Some of the many other flowering plants that grow in the state include azaleas, camellias, dogwoods, violets, pink and white Cherokee roses, crepe myrtles, and green Virginia creeper.

Mississippi National Park Areas

This map shows some of Mississippi's national parks, battlefields, historic parks, and other areas protected by the National Park Service.

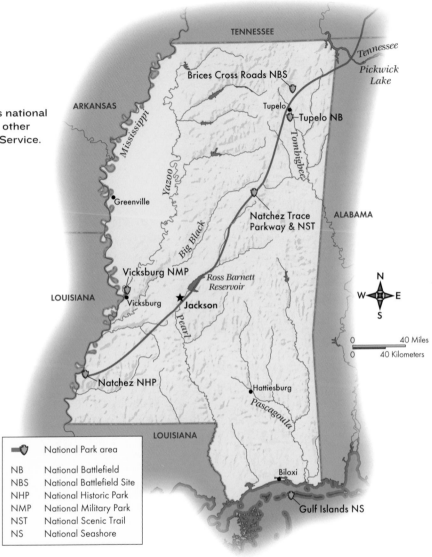

TENNESSEE

Tennessee

Pickwick Lake

Brices Cross Roads NBS

ARKANSAS

Tupelo

Tupelo NB

Mississippi

Yazoo

Tombigbee

Natchez Trace Parkway & NST

ALABAMA

Big Black

Vicksburg NMP

Ross Barnett Reservoir

LOUISIANA

Vicksburg

Jackson

Pearl

N
W   E
S

0 ———— 40 Miles
0 ———— 40 Kilometers

Natchez NHP

Hattiesburg

Pascagoula

LOUISIANA

	National Park area
NB	National Battlefield
NBS	National Battlefield Site
NHP	National Historic Park
NMP	National Military Park
NST	National Scenic Trail
NS	National Seashore

Biloxi

Gulf Islands NS

ANIMAL LIFE

Have you ever seen a nine-banded armadillo? You could spot one in Mississippi. This little critter is one of hundreds of different animal species native to the state. White-tailed deer, cottontail rabbits, raccoons, and squirrels are common. The woods, coastal islands, and backcountry also teem with coyotes, minks, striped skunks, muskrats, and foxes. If you venture into the swampy areas, you might spot the American alligator or the extremely rare Mississippi sandhill crane. Deadly cottonmouths, water moccasins, rattlers, coral snakes, and copperheads make Mississippi their home, too.

Q8 WHY DO SO MANY BIRDS TRAVEL THE MISSISSIPPI FLYWAY?

A8 This route, which begins at the Arctic Coastal Plain and Canada's Mackenzie River and roughly follows the Mississippi River, is perfect for soaring. There are no mountains along the route to cause wind interference, and the numerous rivers, forests, and lakes provide food and protective resting places along the way.

The mockingbird is Mississippi's state bird.

ANIMALS IN DANGER

Much of the animal life that was once plentiful in Mississippi is now rare, owing to a long history of hunting in the area. Although hunting is still popular in the state, it is closely regulated now. Thirty-seven animals are listed as threatened or endangered in Mississippi. A few of the birds on the list include the red-cockaded woodpecker, the brown pelican, the bald eagle, and the beautiful Mississippi sandhill crane. The eastern indigo snake, the gopher tortoise, the American alligator, and several species of turtle are also on the list. Other threatened or endangered mammals in Mississippi include the finback whale, the humpback whale, two species of black bear, and the Indiana bat.

All kinds of birds are found in Mississippi, especially during migration seasons. Some of Mississippi's native birds include the mockingbird, which is the state bird, as well as wrens, hummingbirds, turkeys, quail, wild doves, vultures, and waterfowl of all kinds. The Mississippi Flyway is one of the Northern Hemisphere's major migration routes. About 40 percent of North American waterfowl such as ducks and geese, as well as 326 North American species of birds, take this path through the air. During their migration, thousands of these birds touch down in Mississippi, making the state a bird-watcher's delight.

PROTECTING THE ENVIRONMENT

Take a deep breath! You'll find few states with cleaner air than Mississippi. It's one of only a handful that meet nationally established air quality standards for public health. It also has abundant water resources: about 66,000 acres (27,000 hectares) of tidal wetlands and more than 4 million acres (1.6 million ha) of fresh-water wetlands.

More recently, industrial development has spread throughout Mississippi, resulting in increased pollution of waterways and coastal areas. Additionally, thousands of acres of land, including wetlands, have been converted to industrial areas. But state environmentalists are working hard to make sure that Mississippi's great beauty and vast resources are kept safe.

SEE IT HERE!

SANDHILL CRANE NATIONAL WILDLIFE REFUGE

In southeast Mississippi lives one of the rarest bird species. The Mississippi sandhill crane is a critically endangered bird found nowhere else on earth except in the wet pine **savannahs** of this region. There are only about 100 of these birds left. The majestic cranes stand about 5 feet tall (1.5 m), have a 6-foot (1.8 m) wingspan, and live about 15 to 20 years in the wild. The best time and place to see them is in January and February at the Mississippi Sandhill Crane National Wildlife Refuge in Jackson County.

WORD TO KNOW

savannahs *treeless plains*

MINI-BIO

JACOB M. VALENTINE: FRIEND OF THE SANDHILL CRANE

Jacob M. Valentine (1917–2000) is known as the father of Mississippi's Sandhill Crane National Wildlife Refuge. Early in his career as a Gulf Coast wildlife biologist, Valentine began to investigate how the sandhills were affected by the construction of an interstate highway through their habitat. He soon realized that the cranes were at great risk. His determined efforts brought national attention to the situation. He spent the next 30 years devoting his career to sandhill cranes and the refuge that is their only habitat. Without Valentine, there would be no refuge for these rare birds today.

? **Want to know more?** See www.fws.gov/mississipisandhillcrane/

Sandhill cranes

READ ABOUT

A veiw of
Emerald Mound
near Natchez

**28,000–
10,000 BCE**

*Humans arrive in
North America*

▲ **900–1300 CE**

*The Mississippian
culture is at its height*

1250–1600

*The Natchez build
Emerald Mound*

CHAPTER TWO

FIRST PEOPLE

★

TAKE A ROAD TRIP THROUGH MISSISSIPPI AND YOU'RE LIKELY TO COME ACROSS SEVERAL PLACES WHERE THE GROUND BULGES TO FORM MOUNDS. If these mounds seem unnatural, it's because they were made by people, not Mother Nature. The ancient people who lived in the area built temples and sanctuaries, as well as homes for rulers and religious leaders, on top of the mounds.

1600s
The Natchez decline as the French arrive

1800s
Ancient bones are discovered at Emerald Mound

◄ **1500s**
The Mississippian civilization disappears

THE MISSISSIPPIAN CIVILIZATION

Based on clues they have found, archaeologists think that people came to North America as long as 30,000 years ago. But so far, proof of human life on the continent goes back only 12,000 years. What they do know for sure is that one of the greatest of all ancient North American civilizations thrived throughout the Mississippi region. Archaeologists call this society—you guessed it—the Mississippian civilization.

MISSISSIPPIAN TOWNS AND VILLAGES

The Mississippians established urban centers throughout the middle and southeastern regions of North America that lasted for hundreds of years. In fact, the Mississippian civilization, which came into being in about 700 CE, was one of the longest-surviving civilizations ever to exist on the continent.

Between about 900 and 1300 CE, many large cities flourished between the Atlantic Ocean and present-day

This Mississippian object is a gorget, a piece of armor that protects the throat. It dates from 700 to 1500 CE.

Arkansas and Oklahoma. The Mississippians had a trading network that brought them crystal and mica from the Appalachian Mountains, gold and silver from Canada, and copper and pottery from the Great Lakes region.

Riverbanks were dotted with towns and villages. The towns had homes, broad public squares, and playing fields for ball games. Beyond the towns, Mississippians grew crops of corn and other products in well-tended fields. Highly respected women in each town oversaw the social order. They helped resolve disputes, enforced the laws of society, and acted as spiritual guides and judges.

TEMPLE MOUND BUILDERS

In their impressive temple mounds—some as large as 8 acres (3 ha)—the Mississippian people left archaeologists and historians lots of clues about how they lived. Archaeologists have dug up everything from tools, cookware, and jewelry to masks, carved figures, and peace pipes. But these mounds were not ancient dumps—far from it! They were sacred places reserved for religious rituals and important public events. It was from the temple mounds that the fearsome Great Sun ruled, delivering messages and handing out punishments to the Mississippian people. Though human, the Great Sun wielded absolute control, and all the Mississippian people revered him as a god.

By the 1500s, the vast Mississippian culture of the Southeast had mysteriously disappeared. Only the mounds survived. Some mound-building cultures remained, particularly in what is now Mississippi. These included ancestors of today's Chickasaw, Choctaw, and other smaller groups. These groups would continue to maintain and preserve the earlier ways of life established by the Mississippian culture.

Mississippian shell face

SEE IT HERE!

EMERALD MOUND

Most of the Mississippian mounds are gone now, some wearing away naturally, others bulldozed out of existence. But the state of Mississippi still has several. One is Emerald Mound, northeast of the city of Natchez. Built by the early Natchez sometime between 1250 and 1600, this is the largest mound in the state and the second-largest in the entire country. Its rectangular base measures 435 feet (133 m) by 770 feet (235 m)—an area that covers 8 acres (3 ha)!

Native American Settlements
(Before European Contact)

This map shows the general area of Native American peoples before European settlers arrived.

THE THREE GREAT TRIBES

Look at a map of Mississippi and you'll quickly see that many of its cities, rivers, and roads have Native American names. You may have heard of some of these Native American groups: the Biloxi, the Yazoo, and the Pascagoula. These would later be names of towns and cities in Mississippi.

But the most powerful and largest of Mississippi's early Native American cultures were the Chickasaws, the Choctaws, and the Natchez. Many of their customs and ways of life were similar, but each had its own distinctive culture, as well.

The Chickasaws

The Chickasaws lived across the northern part of what is now Mississippi, mainly in the state's rugged northeastern hills. They were a fierce people who often made slaves of their enemies. Before battle, the men painted their faces and shaved the sides of their heads, leaving only a strip of hair down the middle. The greatest Chickasaw warriors were entitled to wear headdresses of swan feathers.

A *minko*, or chief, led each Chickasaw village, and the head of all the minkos was known as the high minko. Chickasaw society was **matrilineal**, meaning the children became part of their mother's clan rather than their father's. Chickasaw villages were often large, containing a council house, a ceremonial room, a log fort, sports grounds, and other structures. If a Chickasaw town was attacked, every able warrior fought to protect his family, using bows and arrows, knives, and blowguns made of cane, which shot small, deadly arrows.

The Chickasaws did little farming. Their food came mainly from fishing, hunting, and trading with the

SEE IT HERE!

THE SINGING RIVER

If you ever go to the Pascagoula River, you may hear an amazing sound. Some say it is like the sound of a swarm of bees. According to Native American lore, the Pascagoula people joined hands and walked into the river to their death. They did this to avoid being enslaved by the Biloxi. The river sings the death song of of the Pascagoula people.

WORD TO KNOW

matrilineal *relating to tracing a family line through the mother's side*

MUSSACUNNA: CHICKASAW CHIEF

According to legend, Chickasaw chief Mussacunna (dates unknown), meaning "singing winds," was a powerful chief, a great warrior, and a skilled hunter and trader. He made his home in the far northwest corner of Mississippi. Mussacunna had great wealth and was highly successful at raising corn. Even today, locals call the land on which he grew his crop "Mussacunna's corn land." He is buried on the land where he lived, beside a creek that also bears his name.

? Want to know more? See www.rootsweb.com/~msdesoto/chickasaw.html

Choctaws. Well-established extended families had both a circular house used in the winter and a rectangular house used in the summer. They also had buildings for storing corn and other staples. In other buildings, they kept turkeys and chickens.

The Chickasaws believed that life continued after death and that there were good and evil spirits as well as a supreme being, called Ababinili. At death, a Chickasaw's face would be painted red, and he or she would be buried sitting up and facing west.

The Choctaws

The Choctaws lived in the central part of the state. According to Choctaw legend, they and the Chickasaw nation were once united, but at some point became divided. Although they battled

Choctaws perform a dance before the start of a ball game.

each other often, they appeared to be closely related, trading with one another and sharing similar languages and traditions. Like the Chickasaw chieftains, Choctaw leaders were also called minkos.

The Choctaws were far greater in number—and a much more peaceful people—than the Chickasaws. In 1600, the Chickasaw nation had about 5,000 people, whereas the Choctaw had about four times that many. But while the Choctaws always wanted peace rather than war, if enemies attacked, they fought back fearlessly.

The Choctaws depended mostly on farming for their livelihood. For food, they grew beans, melons, pumpkins, and, most importantly, corn. They grew so many crops that they often had plenty left over to sell. They also depended on trade and, later, sold livestock and other goods to the Europeans. Altogether, this made them a prosperous society.

Hunting was another important activity. After the bison in the Southeast were overhunted, deer became the Choctaws' main source of meat. Deer also provided skins for clothing. Besides deer, the Choctaws hunted wild turkeys, raccoons, rabbits, and other small animals, and fished using nets and spears.

The Choctaw territory was vast. It covered more than 23 million acres (9.3 million ha) of land in present-day Mississippi alone!

Picture Yourself . . .

Playing Choctaw Stickball

You join the field, ready to play *ishtaboli*, a version of stickball that resembles today's lacrosse. But there are a lot of players on the field with you. In fact, teams often had 25 to 30 players per side!

The game is rough. Players push, trip, dodge, and even leap over each other. Once you get possession of the ball, you signal your teammates with a shout—"*hokli ho!*" At this cue, your teammates drop their sticks and attack the nearest opponent to keep him from making a move. To win, your team has to score as many as 100 points. If you lose, you're expected to be a good sport. But if you win, your team furiously heckles the losers by gobbling loudly like wild turkeys!

MINI-BIO

A-PUSH-MA-TA-HA-HU-BI: CHOCTAW WARRIOR

A-push-ma-ta-ha-hu-bi, or Pushmataha (1764–1824), was revered as one of the greatest Choctaw warriors ever. His name is said to mean "his arm and all the weapons in his hands are fatal to his foes." Other Native Americans knew him as "the panther's claw." Pushmataha was respected by the white people he encountered, and at the end of his life, he went to Washington, D.C., on a Choctaw business mission to meet with the secretary of war. He died of pneumonia while there, on December 24, 1824. His body is buried in the Washington, D.C., Congressional Cemetery.

❓ **Want to know more?** See www.natchezbelle.org/ahgp-ms/push.htm

The Choctaws enjoyed socializing and were intensely interested in sports such as stickball. They had few religious rituals, but the most important were burial practices. After a Choctaw died, his or her body would be stored in a chest or in a bag made of animal skins and placed in the community's collective bone house. To the Choctaws, the bones of the dead commanded the highest respect. In the autumn of each year, the people held a festival of mourning for the dead. The community opened its sacred mound and buried all the bones from the bone house in it.

People who had been killed by the Chickasaws or a large animal were treated differently. Their bodies were left exactly where they were found and buried under rocks and stones carried to the site by the victims' mothers or wives.

WORD TO KNOW

litter *a cushioned mat or platform attached to poles for carrying a passenger, sometimes curtained for privacy*

The Natchez

The culture thought to be most closely related to the Mississippians was that of the Natchez. Like his Mississippian ancestor, the Natchez leader was also called the Great Sun and was worshipped as a direct descendant of the god of the sun. His people carried him from place to place on a **litter**, so his feet never touched the earth. If he had to walk, servants covered the ground with mats.

The absolute power of the early Natchez rulers was unheard of in other groups in the region. The Great Sun had the final say on every aspect of his subjects' lives and controlled everyone's possessions. The Great Sun also had a female counterpart, the Woman Chief, who had equal power.

Like the Choctaws, the Natchez relied primarily on farming to survive. Natchez social classes were clearly and strictly defined, and a person inherited his or her position within the society from the mother's side of the family. At the top was the royal class, known as the suns. Below them were the nobles, and then the common people. At the bottom were the slaves and captives.

Every Natchez village had its own mound, topped by a temple. Those who did not belong to the royal family lived in houses surrounding the mound. These houses were usually round, well-constructed huts with pointed, tightly woven straw roofs.

By the late 1600s, Natchez culture was well into its decline as European settlements grew. Disturbed by outsiders—first the Spanish and then the French and English—not only the Natchez, but all of Mississippi's Native Americans struggled to maintain their traditional ways of life.

In the early 1800s, near Emerald Mound, someone discovered a human pelvis that turned out to be 5,580 years old. The bones of an extinct ice age sloth—dating back about 17,840 years—were also found!

A hut in a Natchez village

READ ABOUT

Hernando de Soto and his crew encountered the Mississippi River in 1541.

1541
Hernando de Soto and his men arrive in Mississippi

1673
The Marquette and Jolliet expedition enters Mississippi

1682 ▶
René-Robert Cavelier, Sieur de La Salle, enters Mississippi

CHAPTER THREE

EXPLORATION AND SETTLEMENT

★

WHILE MANY TOWNS IN MISSIS-SIPPI HAVE NATIVE AMERICAN NAMES, OTHERS HAVE FRENCH NAMES. The French pushed through the area, forcing out the Native people and establishing many towns. But oppression of Mississippi's Native Americans did not begin with the French. It began with the Spaniards in 1541 when Spanish explorer Hernando de Soto led his well-armed troops into Mississippian lands.

◄ **1699**

Pierre Le Moyne, Sieur d'Iberville, lands near Biloxi

1754

The French and Indian War begins

1776

Americans declare their independence from the British

In 1542, de Soto's expedition was met by Native Americans traveling in canoes.

THE CLASH OF CULTURES

Spanish **conquistador** Hernando de Soto was the first European to travel into the North American inland wilderness. The Spaniards' appearance, with their armor and powerful horses, terrified the Indians, who had never seen horses. The Spaniards' brutal actions and demands, however, angered the Native peoples, and they fought back. Chickasaw warriors fought de Soto for four months, driving him away in April 1541.

De Soto's army reached the Mississippi River in May 1541, making them the first Europeans to come upon the river. De Soto never found the riches he sought in North America. He died of a fever on the banks of the river near present-day Natchez, Mississippi, in 1542.

After de Soto's death, his troops sailed down the Mississippi and then on to Cuba. But their getaway was not easy. The Natchez pursued them in 100 brightly painted, canopied canoes moving in battle formation until the Spanish entered the Gulf of Mexico. De Soto's mission ended at last on July 18, 1543.

European Exploration of Mississippi

The colored arrows on this map show the routes taken by European explorers between 1541 and 1699.

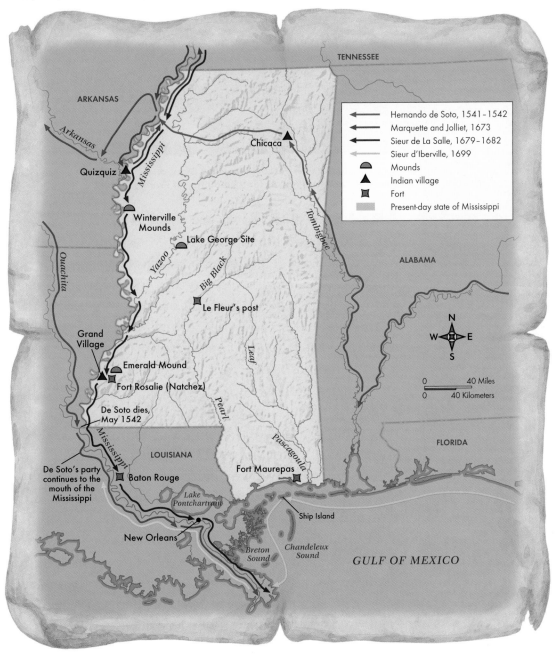

TENNESSEE

ARKANSAS

Arkansas

Chicaca

Quizquiz

Mississippi

Winterville Mounds

Lake George Site

Yazoo

Big Black

Tombigbee

ALABAMA

Ouachita

Le Fleur's post

Grand Village

Emerald Mound

Fort Rosalie (Natchez)

Leaf

De Soto dies, May 1542

Pearl

Pascagoula

De Soto's party continues to the mouth of the Mississippi

Mississippi

LOUISIANA

FLORIDA

Baton Rouge

Fort Maurepas

Lake Pontchartrain

Ship Island

New Orleans

Breton Sound

Chandeleux Sound

GULF OF MEXICO

Legend:
- Hernando de Soto, 1541–1542
- Marquette and Jolliet, 1673
- Sieur de La Salle, 1679–1682
- Sieur d'Iberville, 1699
- Mounds
- Indian village
- Fort
- Present-day state of Mississippi

0   40 Miles
0   40 Kilometers

THE GREAT SUN OF THE NATCHEZ

Quigaltam was the Great Sun of the Natchez at the time Hernando de Soto was making his way through the southeastern Native American lands. The center of Quigaltam's kingdom, near today's Greenville, was also called Quigaltam. The Spaniards reported that Quigaltam's largest town had 500 houses, a huge number at the time, and between 30,000 and 40,000 military troops. Quigaltam himself had a striking appearance. In accordance with Natchez rituals, his forehead had been flattened during infancy. His body was tattooed with elaborate designs in red, blue, and black.

Most of the details of the leader's life are now lost, but one was vividly recorded by the Spanish. On his deathbed, de Soto commanded Quigaltam to make an appearance at the Spanish encampment. De Soto sent word that he was a "Great Sun" himself and must be obeyed. The mighty Natchez monarch laughed him off, telling his messengers that if de Soto were really a god, let him dry up the Mississippi River. Then, Quigaltam said, he might believe it and show up.

WORD TO KNOW

missionary *a person who spreads faith and religion to others*

French explorer René-Robert Cavelier, Sieur de La Salle, claiming the entire region for the country of France in 1682

ARRIVAL OF THE FRENCH

For 130 years after de Soto, Mississippi's Native Americans were left in relative peace. They sometimes fought among themselves, but they were free from the torture, theft, and enslavement brought by Europeans. In the late 1600s, however, Europeans again ventured into Mississippi lands, coming from the north down the Mississippi River.

The first of these, in 1673, were seven French explorers led by Father Jacques Marquette, a Roman Catholic **missionary**, and Louis Jolliet, an agent of the French government. Their expedition, begun in the Great Lakes, took them down the river to where Rosedale, Mississippi, is today. They spent little time there, and returned north.

In 1682, Frenchman René-Robert Cavelier, Sieur de La Salle arrived, also by way of the Mississippi River. La Salle boldly claimed all the land of the entire Mississippi basin for the French king, Louis XIV. Named Louisiana, the territory reached far beyond the borders of today's state of Louisiana. Disliked by many of his fellow Frenchmen, La Salle was, however, admired by Native Americans. He befriended Mississippi's Natchez peoples and met their Great Sun, with whom he smoked the calumet, or peace pipe. But problems with his countrymen continued. In 1687, **mutineers** within La Salle's own expedition ambushed and killed him. He died without creating a single settlement.

EUROPEAN SETTLEMENT

In 1699, a French Canadian named Pierre Le Moyne, Sieur d'Iberville, landed on Mississippi's Gulf Coast near today's city of Biloxi. King Louis XIV had commissioned him to secure the mouth of the Mississippi River for France. The settlement that Iberville established, Fort Maurepas, was located at what is now Ocean Springs.

Fort Maurepas was the first European settlement in the Lower Mississippi Valley. The area around Fort Maurepas was not fertile and farming was almost impossible. Famine was a constant problem. Many settlers died of **dysentery** and perhaps **malaria**. French settlers abandoned the region in 1702.

Iberville's younger brother, Jean Baptiste Le Moyne, Sieur de Bienville, started a second settlement in 1716. He built Fort Rosalie on the banks of the Mississippi River, in the midst of Natchez lands. As the colony grew, it became a prosperous town and its name was changed to Natchez.

With Fort Rosalie, and another colony built in 1718, the Natchez were being invaded from all sides. The French colonists built homes, marked off farmland, and began raising crops. The Natchez rarely moved against them. But their dissatisfaction was mounting.

WORD TO KNOW

allies *people who are on the same side in a conflict*

Today, Natchez is the site of the oldest settlement established by white explorers that is still in existence within the state of Mississippi!

Q8 WHAT WAS THE FRENCH AND INDIAN WAR ABOUT?

A8 It was a struggle for the control of North American lands and trading rights. The British, along with colonial American soldiers, fought against the French and their Native American allies. Battles took place from Canada to the Gulf Coast. After nine long years, the British defeated their enemies. The war ended in 1763.

CONFLICT WITH THE FRENCH

The Chickasaws were an undefeated nation. Their power was widespread and legendary. The Natchez were their **allies**, and they were on friendly terms with British traders throughout their lands. Relations with the French remained cautious. In 1720, the French governor insisted that the Chickasaws stop trading with the British. The Chickasaws ignored this demand, and war broke out with the French. The Chickasaws won, and the French couldn't break the British-Chickasaw alliance. Frustrated, the French allied with the Choctaws, promising guns in exchange for Chickasaw scalps.

Although the Natchez were strong, their hopeless battle against French rule finally ruined them. In 1729, the Natchez attacked Fort Rosalie, killing more than 300 and kidnapping another 400. The French abandoned their settlement on the edges of Natchez territory. But the attacks sent them into a final fury. A French army arrived within two years and destroyed the remaining Natchez. By 1732, the last Natchez survivors had merged with the Chickasaws and the Choctaws.

In 1736, the French sent 1,600 troops against the Chickasaws. For 34 years, the French repeatedly attacked the Chickasaws, often helped by the Choctaws, but the Chickasaw nation always prevailed. By 1754, the year that marked the start of the French and Indian War, French forces barely existed in Mississippi.

During the nine years of war, France lost ground in the Southeast. In the end, the British controlled all the land east of the Mississippi River except New Orleans. The territory was divided in half. The southern portion of Mississippi, including the Natchez settlement, was absorbed into the British province of South Florida. The northern half merged with Georgia Territory.

On July 4, 1776, American colonists declared independence from the British. The Revolutionary War, which had begun the year before, officially ended in 1783, and the United States was born.

Mississippi as we know it today was not even a territory belonging to the United States. By the 1790s, only about 4,500 non-Native Americans lived in the 48,430 square miles (125,4334 sq km) of today's Mississippi.

Over the years, there had been many conflicts between the French and the Native Americans throughout the region. New settlements were built as Native communities were forced out. With railroads and other economic developments on the horizon, along with a wave of new immigrants, Mississippi was about to change forever.

Picture Yourself . . .

Leaving Home for the Wilderness

Imagine homesteading in the wilderness. There, with no dwelling yet, you might live outside for days, or even months, regardless of the weather. You would have to clear enough land to build on—meaning chopping down trees, getting rid of bushes, and digging and hauling rocks from the ground. Then, of course, you'd have to build your house, not to mention furniture!

At some point, you'd have to stop and look for food. That would mean learning how to hunt and fish and how to tell good-to-eat wild plants from poisonous ones. Once your garden grew in, you'd have to hope the weather didn't destroy your crops. And depending on whether you had the chance to trade, you might have to make all your own clothes and tools. But at least you'd know you could take care of yourself!

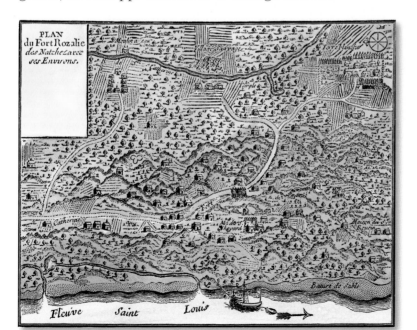

This map of Fort Rosalie, which lay on the Mississippi River in the Natchez region, dates to the 1700s.

1812–1814

The War of 1812 is fought

▲1817

Mississippi becomes the 20th state

1820

The Choctaws agree to the Treaty of Doak's Stand

CHAPTER FOUR

GROWTH AND CHANGE

★

B Y 1776, THE FRENCH HAD GIVEN THEIR LAND ALONG THE MISSISSIPPI TO THE SPANISH. The hardships of the frontier were too much for the French, and keeping the land was impossible. On the east side of the river, Natchez was again the center of the white population. But there were barely more than 1,000 settlers, most of English descent.

1861–1865

The Civil War is fought

1863

The Union takes control of Vicksburg

1870 ►

Hiram Revels becomes the first African American U.S. senator

THE EFFECTS OF THE REVOLUTION

During the Revolutionary War, most trappers, traders, scouts, and Native Americans in Mississippi sided with the colonists, while settlers in the region tended to be loyal to the British. Still, the war seemed far away, and their land was in the hands of the Spanish. A bigger concern for Mississippi settlers was survival. Most people were struggling to make life on the frontier work.

It wasn't long before the new United States began taking an interest in the Mississippi River and its surrounding regions. By 1797, Spain gave up the Natchez district and much of the rest of its land to the new nation. By 1798, the U.S. Congress had created the Mississippi Territory, and growth was on the horizon.

MIGRATION TO MISSISSIPPI

Early in the 1800s, two major migrations into Mississippi Territory occurred. The first migration began the year the territory was established, with settlers from Alabama, Georgia, and the Carolinas making their way west.

In the late 1800s, many settlers loaded up their wagons and moved into Mississippi.

Mississippi: From Territory to Statehood

This map shows the original Mississippi Territory and the area (in yellow) that became the state of Mississippi in 1817.

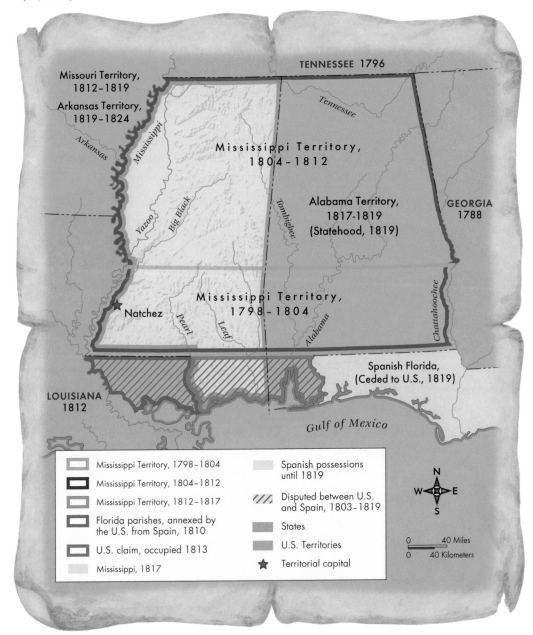

Missouri Territory, 1812–1819

Arkansas Territory, 1819–1824

TENNESSEE 1796

Arkansas

Mississippi

Tennessee

Mississippi Territory, 1804–1812

Alabama Territory, 1817-1819 (Statehood, 1819)

GEORGIA 1788

Yazoo

Big Black

Tombighee

Chattahoochee

★ Natchez

Pearl

Leaf

Alabama

Mississippi Territory, 1798–1804

Spanish Florida, (Ceded to U.S., 1819)

LOUISIANA 1812

Gulf of Mexico

Legend:

- Mississippi Territory, 1798–1804
- Mississippi Territory, 1804–1812
- Mississippi Territory, 1812–1817
- Florida parishes, annexed by the U.S. from Spain, 1810
- U.S. claim, occupied 1813
- Mississippi, 1817
- Spanish possessions until 1819
- Disputed between U.S. and Spain, 1803–1819
- States
- U.S. Territories
- ★ Territorial capital

N W E S

0   40 Miles
0   40 Kilometers

In 1816, one settler counted 4,000 people coming into Mississippi in only nine days!

WORD TO KNOW

yeomen *people who cultivate a small farm*

In 1812, war broke out between the United States and Great Britain. Migration slowed until the war's end in December 1814. But then "Mississippi fever" struck hard. Thousands of settlers came. In 1817, Mississippi became the 20th state, and by 1819, migration decreased.

Most settlers came from the states of North and South Carolina and other bordering regions. Almost all of them were of Scots-Irish heritage. Those who settled in the eastern and middle parts of the state pushed out the Chickasaws and Choctaws. They became fiercely independent backwoods farmers, called **yeomen**.

Many settlers were drawn to Natchez, the territory's largest population center and capital. Others settled in Mississippi's fertile Delta. With the region's abundant natural resources, the settlers saw a bright future. And with few Natchez Indians left, many settlers bought large tracts of land. They leapt at the opportunity to own vast wealth-producing plantations.

Throughout the state, the new residents engaged in agriculture. Industrial work held little interest for them. Agriculture shaped Mississippi from its beginnings and for the next 200 years.

THE ISSUE OF SLAVERY

By the 1790s, a number of wealthy landowners farmed the Natchez area. Their fortunes came mainly from tobacco, the first profitable crop in the South. Others prospered by growing indigo, a plant used for making blue dye. But neither of these plants had long-term promise.

Cotton, however, was in big demand, especially in England. But separating the cotton fiber from the bolls (seedpods) and sticky seeds took hours. This changed in 1793 when Eli Whitney invented a cotton gin, which easily extracted the cotton fiber. Plantation owners pounced on the cotton gin. Soon, Natchez planters were building gins and planting cotton. By the time of statehood in 1817, Mississippi was awash in cotton.

This development brought the need for thousands of more workers. Mississippi plantation owners used forced or slave labor to meet that need. Indentured Africans had been brought to the American colonies since the 1600s, both in the North and South. But it wasn't until 1719 that the first enslaved workers were brought to Mississippi from the West Indies. Most enslaved workers ended up in the Natchez district.

By the 1830s, the Natchez region had become the center of the cotton-growing world. It was home to more than half of the country's millionaires by the 1850s. These plantation owners could not have maintained their lifestyles without the backbreaking labor of the enslaved workers.

These workers are ginning cotton, which is the process of removing the cotton fiber from the seedpods. The invention of the cotton gin helped make cotton a hugely profitable crop in Mississippi.

INDIAN REMOVAL

As more slaves were brought to the state, other people were pushed out. Mississippi settlers eyed the huge territory of the Choctaw and the Chickasaw nations. By 1820, white settlers lived on one-third of Mississippi's land, and the Indians claimed the other two-thirds.

LOSING THEIR LAND

In getting the Native Americans to leave the land, the U.S. government used bribery, false promises, and outright military threats. They began by giving Native Americans huge amounts of food and liquor. When the bribes didn't work, the government promised them millions of acres in what is now Arkansas. And when Native peoples still did not agree to move, the U.S. government threatened to use the army to forcibly remove them. Mississippi's legislature enacted laws that took away all Indian rights and made U.S. claims to the land theoretically legal.

In 1835 alone, the U.S. government sold 3 million acres (1 million ha) of land in Mississippi, at only $1.25 an acre!

In three aggressive pushes, agents of the government forced treaties on the Native Americans, which removed them from their ancient homelands. The first was the 1820 Treaty of Doak's Stand. Through direct threats and offers of land in Arkansas and Indian Territory (present-day Oklahoma), the Choctaws were forced from central Mississippi. But thousands of Chickasaws and Choctaws still lived in the north and east.

In the 1830 Treaty of Dancing Rabbit Creek, the Choctaws surrendered their remaining territory. Two years later, the Chickasaws also gave up, under the Treaty of Pontotoc Creek. By 1832, Indian removal was complete. Native Americans were driven, mostly on foot, to Indian Territory. This journey, during which some 4,000 Indians died, is known by many Indian nations as the Trail of Tears. For white Mississippi settlers, it meant almost 6 million acres (2 million ha) of cheap land to homestead.

Many white settlers became cotton farmers. Others bought and resold lands for large profits. Between 1830 and 1840, Mississippi's white population increased 175 percent, and its enslaved black population rose 197 percent. Mississippi had its biggest population explosion in its history.

PLANTATION SOCIETY

Mississippi's black population explosion was very different from the white population boom. Whites came to prosper; blacks were forced to help them. Slaves worked in fields or as dockhands, maids, and factory workers. Field slaves, including women and children, generally worked from sunrise to sunset, with a short pause for lunch. Children were sent into the fields as early as age six or seven. Slaves had no legal rights, not

Picking cotton was difficult work. Enslaved workers spent long days picking cotton for no pay.

even to get married. They were sold at auctions, willed to owners' relatives, or traded for horses and cows.

Enslaved people worked hard and without pay. They had no reason to work hard other than earning a reward, such as a day pass to visit a family member, or avoiding a punishment, such as a public beating. Enslaved families struggled to live in dignity. Some tried to escape, but Free States, where slavery was illegal, were far away. From 1826 to 1860, Mississippi had four unsuccessful slave rebellions, which resulted in legislators and owners imposing stricter controls.

In the beginning, planters tried to justify slavery by claiming that the Southern economy would collapse without it. By the 1830s, planters insisted that slavery was "good" for everyone. For people from Africa and the West Indies, they claimed, it brought civilization and Christianity. And for planters, it produced profits that allowed them to enjoy mansions, servants, and, for some, political power. Most slave owners had fewer

NO JUSTICE

William Johnson was a free man of color, one of about 500 living in Natchez before the Civil War. He was wealthy enough to own 1,000 acres (400 ha) of land, three barbershops, and at least a dozen slaves. In 1851, Johnson was murdered by a white man over a land dispute. But because the only witnesses to the crime were African Americans, his murderer was not brought to trial. No person of color could testify in court against a white person. Sometimes crimes against whites went unpunished because the only witnesses were not white.

WORD TO KNOW

doctrine *a principle that is taught, or a system of belief*

than 50 slaves, but the tiny minority who owned 500 or more had huge plantations and used their wealth to dominate state politics.

The planters' defense of slavery rested on the ideas that black people were inferior to whites and that slavery was their natural condition. According to this **doctrine**, called white supremacy, enslavement of blacks improved and civilized them.

Under this system, few Mississippians were entirely free. Slaveholders, knowing their slaves' anger could erupt at any moment, carried arms. Planters sheltered their wives and daughters from the harsh conditions of slave life, fearing that women would speak out against the cruelty or try to educate the slaves. Teaching enslaved people to read or write was illegal.

Poor whites could not escape poverty because planters filled jobs with enslaved people. So whites had fewer jobs and lower pay. They lived in log cabins and raised chickens, hogs, and vegetables. Many of them left and headed west. Those who remained acted as if they were better than blacks and saw the slaveholders as their allies. Ironically, these attitudes led them to defend the practice that was keeping them poor. White supremacy gave planters the loyalty of the white majority that they needed to keep slaves from finding allies and gaining freedom. It made slavery a system that held down millions of slaves and many more white people.

A NATION DIVIDED

In 1848, the United States won half of Mexico's territory in a war over Texas. Northern states wanted the new territories to be free, whereas Southern states wanted them to have the right to choose slavery. By the 1850s, the issue divided them deeply. In 1860, Abraham

Lincoln was a presidential candidate who wanted to prevent slavery from spreading to the West. When he won the election, Mississippi slave owners and others saw him as a threat to slavery and states' rights. They favored **secession** and starting a separate country for slave states (known as the Confederacy).

Mississippians were divided over leaving the Union. Slaves, of course, wanted freedom. Poor whites knew they would do most of the fighting and dying. Some rich planters opposed a war that might disturb their profits. There also were "Unionists" in Mississippi who opposed secession and war. But pro-Confederacy "fire-eaters" had the loudest voice and the most delegates at the 1861 convention that voted 84 to 15 to secede. U.S. senator Jefferson Davis of Mississippi, a leading slaveholder who had held many state offices, became president of the Confederacy.

Jefferson Davis (left of the table), a Mississippi senator, became the president of the Confederacy. He is shown here with his advisers.

WORD TO KNOW

secession *the withdrawal from a group or organization*

The Union army took control of Vicksburg in May 1863. It was a key victory for General Ulysses S. Grant and his troops.

War fever swept Mississippi, and 78,000 Mississippians marched off to fight for slavery, independence, and white supremacy. Tens of thousands of enslaved Mississippians took advantage of the absence of young white men to escape and join the Union Army.

THE CIVIL WAR

Confederate forces at Fort Sumter, South Carolina, fired the first shots of the Civil War on April 12, 1861. Union general Ulysses S. Grant soon turned his attention to Mississippi, because it lay along the strategic Mississippi River. It was also the home state of the president of the Confederacy. Mississippi became a prime target of the Union forces.

Two railroads intersected in Corinth in the northwest portion of the state. The battle of Corinth in 1862 secured Union control of these railroads.

Located on bluffs above the Mississippi and Yazoo rivers, Vicksburg was strategically key. Grant wanted to capture Vicksburg to give Union forces control of the Mississippi River and to batter Confederates present at Vicksburg and in central Mississippi. The South would thus be divided and weakened.

The campaign to take Vicksburg lasted more than a year. In May 1863, Grant won battles at Port Gibson, Raymond, Jackson, Champion Hill, and the Big Black River.

On May 19 and again on May 22, Grant's forces stormed the Confederate defenses at Vicksburg. They failed each time. On May 23, Grant began the **siege** of Vicksburg. Union forces completely blockaded the city. On July 4, 1863, the Confederate Army surrendered. Vicksburg and the Mississippi River were now under the control of Union forces.

In all, 772 battles and skirmishes took place in Mississippi. More than one-third of Mississippi's soldiers died in battle or of disease. Thousands more were wounded. The Civil War finally ended in 1865, weeks after Confederate general Robert E. Lee surrendered at Appomattox, Virginia. Now efforts would be spent on healing and rebuilding both the country and Mississippi.

JEFFERSON DAVIS: PRESIDENT OF THE CONFEDERACY

Jefferson Davis (1808–1889) was born in Kentucky, but grew up in Mississippi, where he was homeschooled before going to the U.S. Military Academy at West Point. Born into a family of exceptional military men, Davis followed in their footsteps. He was a brilliant leader in battle during the Mexican War of 1846–1848. He also served as a U.S. congressman and a U.S. senator. He resigned his senate office to become president of the Confederate States of America. In 1865, Davis was captured and was sure he would be executed for treason. But after two years in jail, he was released. Before he died in 1888, he called for reconciliation between Northerners and Southerners.

? Want to know more? See http://jeffersondavis.rice.edu/

WORD TO KNOW

siege *a military strategy in which a city or fortress is surrounded, cutting off supplies, and repeatedly attacked until the enemy surrenders*

This school in Vicksburg was created for newly freed slaves after the Civil War.

WORD TO KNOW

vagrancy *the condition of wandering from place to place, lacking a home and money*

AFTER THE WAR

At the end of the war, Mississippi was in chaos. Confederate money was worthless, trade had stopped, and food and clothing were scarce. With slavery gone and the state government in collapse, white violence rose. The all-white delegates at Mississippi's 1865 state constitutional convention abolished slavery but refused to grant rights to former slaves. The battle over human rights began.

The state legislature permitted former slaves to sue or testify in courts, and it legalized their marriages. But it passed Black Codes saying that ex-slaves had to have a home and job or face arrest for **vagrancy**. Blacks were forbidden to own guns or rent land or to marry white people. A new kind of slavery returned to Mississippi.

The U.S. government responded by placing Mississippi and other Southern states under military control. This period is called Reconstruction. The U.S. Congress demanded that Mississippi hold a new state constitutional convention in which black men would vote. In 1867, under the protection of U.S. troops, more black people in Mississippi registered to vote than did white people. At the constitutional convention, 17 black delegates met 83 white delegates, and together they passed Mississippi's most democratic constitution. It granted equal citizenship to all men regardless of property or race. It increased rights for poor whites and women and began the state's public school system.

A new day dawned in Mississippi, with black sheriffs, teachers, congressmen, judges, and landowners. Black and white children played together. Mississippi legislators voted to increase government services and build schools, hospitals, bridges, and railroads. Mississippi's **Civil Rights** Act banned **discrimination** in public buildings and transportation.

Racists responded with fury at what they called black domination, even though 62 of 74 sheriffs were white and only Natchez had a black mayor. Whites controlled the governorship, both houses of the legislature, and the legal system. There were, however, two black lieutenant governors, a black secretary of state, and a black speaker of the house.

Former Confederate soldiers joined the Ku Klux Klan (KKK), angry whites who sometimes used violence and intimidation to restore white supremacy. Bands of Klansmen burned down black schools and churches, and night riders intimidated or killed dozens of black officeholders, voters, and their white allies.

WORDS TO KNOW

civil rights *the basic rights of every citizen*

discrimination *unfair treatment of a person or group*

After white riots in 1875 and 1876, most people who favored equality had been silenced, killed, or driven from the state. The next year, all U.S. troops were withdrawn from the South, and white supremacy returned to Mississippi. The brief experiment in liberty and justice for all ended.

TURN OF THE CENTURY

In Mississippi, the 20th century began with tremendous growth. Over the first 20 years, money was put into a school system that had practically been nonexistent during slavery. Institutions for the disabled

An early 20th-century schoolhouse in Bay St. Louis, Mississippi

opened, and more attention was given to the needs of the poor—but not to all those in need.

Two powerful governors during these early decades were James Kimble Vardaman and Theodore Gilmore Bilbo. These men talked a good deal about **reforms** for the poor and socially disadvantaged—so long as they were white. Both Vardaman and Bilbo were racists, whose ambitious ideas ignored the 60 percent of Mississippi's population who were black and extremely poor.

Neither cared that by keeping African Americans poor and powerless, Mississippians would remain locked in poverty and suffering. With the end of Bilbo's last term, Mississippi's reform trend ended. The state had gone from a land of plenty where "King Cotton" ruled to a place of poverty.

Almost 90 percent of the population lived in rural areas. Blacks and poor whites labored as sharecroppers, working a landowner's fields in return for a place to live and a small amount of the profits from the crops. Most sharecroppers had little hope of ever being free from financial worries.

Whatever progress had been made, it did not benefit Mississippi's poor whites or African Americans. On the contrary, white supremacy and slavery had essentially been restored. By the late 1920s, Mississippi had missed the economic progress that the rest of the United States enjoyed. Despite this, the state would work hard to get back on the right track and strive for democracy, modernity, and opportunity.

WORD TO KNOW

reforms *changes to improve something*

POSTWAR PROGRESS

Big changes were in store for African Americans after the Civil War. Robert Gleed, who had escaped from his Virginia slave owner, lived in Columbus, Mississippi. During Reconstruction, he owned a large farm and opened a general store. He served as president of the Mercantile Land and Banking Company and was head of the Lowndes County Chamber of Commerce. He was also elected to the Mississippi state senate and served two terms.

On a national level, Hiram Revels made history. This college-educated minister and schoolteacher had been a chaplain for a black Union regiment in Mississippi. Once the war was over, Jefferson Davis's place in the U.S. Senate was open. Revel took Davis's spot, becoming the first African American to serve in the U.S. Senate (1870–1871). His campaign message was this: "While I was in favor of building up the colored race, I was not in favor of tearing down the white race. . . . [T]he white race need not be harmed in order to build up the colored race."

These men stood as symbols of the changing times and the opportunities that lay ahead for African Americans.

1927
The Mississippi River floods the Delta

▲**1931**
Cotton prices fall drastically

1940s
Approximately 400,000 people leave Mississippi

CHAPTER FIVE

MORE MODERN TIMES

★

DURING THE 1920S, THE UNITED STATES ENJOYED GREAT WEALTH. After World War I (1914–1918) ended, the country had begun an age of economic prosperity. Mississippi saw progress, as well. Lumber companies logged forests to help build new railroads. Plans for highways across the state were in place. But Mississippi had many issues to solve.

▲ **1962**
James Meredith enrolls at the University of Mississippi

1964
Freedom Summer takes place

2006
The "Mississippi, Believe It" campaign is launched

DISASTER AND THE GREAT DEPRESSION

The Roaring Twenties was a lively decade, sometimes called the Jazz Age. But, during this time, Mississippi struggled with poverty and racial problems. Most Mississippians were barely getting by. Racial violence, poverty, and oppression were part of everyday life.

In 1927, disaster struck the Delta. The Mississippi overflowed its banks, causing the worst flooding in the state's history. Hundreds of millions of dollars worth of property and cotton crops were lost. At least 100,000 people fled their homes.

Mississippians were still struggling when, in October 1929, the U.S. stock market crashed. Many banks and businesses were instantly wiped out. Wealthy people who had lost money could no longer afford to buy freely. This put factory workers and other employees out of work, so they no longer had money, either. Many lost their homes.

The stock market crash was one factor that caused the Great Depression. Mississippians were especially hard-hit because of the state's cotton industry. By 1931, cotton prices had fallen drastically, which was disastrous for the state. The Depression affected the entire nation and lasted throughout the 1930s. Through this experience, however, Mississippians realized that farming alone would not provide for them. The state needed new industries and more jobs.

MAKING CHANGES

By the late 1930s, factories were being built and Mississippi's forestry industry was growing. Petroleum was also discovered in two areas north of Jackson. Overall, however, little had changed—politically, racially, or economically—since 1840.

During World War II, these women worked as welders for a shipbuidling company in Pascagoula.

During World War II (1939–1945), Mississippi's shipbuilding and other businesses boomed as the need for ships and other war supplies increased. Women entered the workforce and kept factories humming while men served as soldiers. Thousands of Mississippians enlisted in the armed forces after the United States entered the war. Away from Mississippi, these young people got a look at what life was like beyond their insulated world.

Between 1940 and 1945, Mississippians' average income rose. But most opportunities were given to whites. Mississippi's African Americans continued to struggle with poverty and lack of equal opportunities.

Since the end of the Civil War, many Mississippians had headed north in search of jobs and better lives. They migrated to Chicago, Detroit, and other big cities. During the 1940s, however, this outpouring greatly increased, with almost 400,000 people moving elsewhere. Of these, about 75 percent were black.

During World War II, many African Americans served as soldiers. These troops are participating in a ceremony in Italy.

WORD TO KNOW

segregation *the act of separating people based on race or class*

After World War II, racial relations began to shift. Many African Americans had fought in the war. Others had gotten jobs in factories and other industries, especially in cities where white workers had left to enlist in the military. During the war, President Franklin D. Roosevelt had taken steps to root out racial discrimination in the military. He had also supported absentee voting by soldiers, which meant that white Mississippians could not keep black soldiers from voting.

In Mississippi, this caused whites to fear losing their control. Black veterans came home wanting more rights. They were dissatisfied with the racial inequality and **segregation** in Mississippi. The U.S. government and people outside of the state were calling for greater racial equality. White Mississippians saw their ways of doing things under attack. For the next 20 years, white Mississippians struggled to keep their power. But this time, the entire nation was watching.

THE CIVIL RIGHTS ERA

In 1954, the United States Supreme Court ruled unanimously against segregation in a monumental case, *Brown v. Board of Education*. The court declared that segregated schools were illegal. Shock waves rippled through Mississippi, which had been operating on a "separate but equal" basis. (The idea was that blacks and whites attended separate schools, but that the schools were supposed to be of equal quality.) Again, the state's white civilians and lawmakers loudly declared that they would never follow the law and would resort to violence if anyone tried to force them to do so.

Segregationists used one law after another to keep Mississippi from changing. In 1956, the legislature repealed, or overturned, the law requiring school attendance for children age 6 to 14. If young people did not have to go to school at all, then **integration** was not even an issue.

In about 1956, the Mississippi State Sovereignty Commission was formed. This state agency spied on both black and white racial "troublemakers" and worked closely with the KKK. Its formation was another sign that African American rights were being abused.

One of the most momentous events in Mississippi's history was the murder of Emmett Till in 1955. Till was a 14-year-old Chicago boy who was visiting his grandfather. He was killed by a group of whites for whistling at a white woman. This brutal murder was publicized in national newspapers. The case spotlighted Mississippi's racial violence for the first time and sparked the civil rights movement.

Still, Mississippi lawmakers and other groups managed to keep segregationist practices alive. Many whites were hardened against integration and feared social change. Then, suddenly, white supremacy began to collapse.

WORD TO KNOW

integration *the bringing together of all members of society as equals*

JAMES MEREDITH: CIVIL RIGHTS PIONEER

James Meredith (1933–), born in Kosciusko, joined the U.S. Air Force at age 18. After nine years in the military, he attended Jackson State College, a school for African Americans. He risked his life to enroll at the University of Mississippi (Ole Miss) in Oxford, an all-white school, in 1962. Later, Meredith organized a civil rights walk from Memphis, Tennessee, to Jackson, Mississippi, called the Walk Against Fear. He was shot during the march but recovered and continued on with his civil rights work. Meredith has written a book about his experiences at Ole Miss as well as a history of Mississippi.

? Want to know more? See www.jfklibrary.org/meredith/jm.html

INTEGRATION

The first big blow came in 1962. A black man named James Meredith wanted to attend the all-white University of Mississippi, known as Ole Miss. A federal court ordered the state to admit him, but Governor Ross Barnett refused. Barnett, a Klan member since the 1920s, was one of the state's most outspoken racists. Protests and violent riots broke out, and rioters attacked Meredith's defenders at Ole Miss. U.S. marshals and soldiers were injured, damage to property was great, and two people were killed.

For his safety, Meredith was escorted on campus by U.S. deputy marshals, forcing Ole Miss to register him as a student. Because of threats on his life, U.S. marshals and sheriffs guarded him the entire time until he graduated. Mississippi's violent reaction to Meredith again brought the state to the nation's attention.

In 1964, integration spread, with similar resistance, to the state's other public schools. Many Mississippi whites supported segregation to the point of using violence to maintain it. In the end, their extreme tactics sped up integration and racial equality in the state. Many people had accepted the coming of integration, but they hadn't said or done anything to help it along.

These silent whites, as well as the entire nation, were shocked by a racially motivated murder in 1963. Medgar Evers, a young African American from Jackson, was the head of the Mississippi chapter of the National Association for the Advancement of Colored People (NAACP). Evers had pledged the organization's resources to help Meredith and others. In June 1963, Evers was shot in the back and killed just outside his house. His murderer, Byron De La Beckwith, was tried twice, but the all-white juries did not convict him. Only in 1994 was he finally retried and convicted of the murder.

FREEDOM SUMMER

Evers's murder inspired 1,000 white volunteers to come to Mississippi the next summer. In violation of segregation laws, they worked and lived with black Mississippians. They worked on a project called Freedom Summer to enroll almost 2,000 African American voters. Freedom Schools taught children about their rights and history.

One June night, KKK members killed three of these young people: Michael Schwerner and Andrew Goodman, white New Yorkers, and James Chaney, a black Mississippian. The three, however, did not lose their lives in vain. Freedom Summer showed that blacks and whites could cooperate on community projects. The murders prodded Congress to pass the landmark 1964 Civil Rights Act.

MEDGAR EVERS: NONVIOLENT ACTIVIST

Medgar Evers (1925–1963) was born near Decatur and fought in the Normandy invasion during World War II. As a student at Alcorn State University, he played football, joined the debate team and the choir, and edited the student newspaper. After graduating from Alcorn, he was turned down when he applied to the all-white University of Mississippi Law School. Sparked by an interest in civil rights, he became the first leader of the Mississippi chapter of the NAACP and organized some of Jackson's earliest protests for equality. In 1962, Evers was crucial in helping James Meredith gain admission to Ole Miss. After he was gunned down in his driveway in 1963 by Byron De La Beckwith, a white supremacist, Evers's brother Charles took his place as head of the NAACP in Mississippi.

? **Want to know more?** See www.africawithin.com/ bios/medgar_evers.htm

64

FANNIE LOU HAMER: CIVIL RIGHTS HEROINE

Fannie Lou Hamer (1917–1977), spent most of her life in the poverty-stricken Mississippi Delta. In 1962, she was fired from her job for attempting to register to vote. She became a civil rights leader and was an organizer of the Student Nonviolent Coordinating Committee (SNCC). Hamer was jailed and beaten for her activities. She founded Freedom Farms Corporation to help African Americans get farmland and was one of the founding members of the Mississippi Freedom Democratic Party. She tried to run for Congress in the 1960s, but whites refused to put her name on the ballot. Later, mock elections showed she would have won if she had had the chance. By the end of her life, Hamer was nationally known and respected.

? Want to know more? See www.africawithin.com/bios/fannie_hamer.htm

THE TURNING TIDES

In autumn 1964, some Mississippi schools were finally integrated. In 1969, the U.S. Supreme Court ruled that all public schools must integrate. Another court order forced the issue in Mississippi, where 33 school districts were holding out. Some whites avoided this ruling by opening private schools for white students only.

In 1969, Charles Evers, the elder brother of Medgar Evers, was elected mayor of Fayette. He became Mississippi's first African American mayor since Reconstruction. He served from 1969 to 1981 and from 1985 to 1989.

A big part of the change in racial attitudes stemmed from economic needs. If Mississippi had kept segregation, its federal funding would have been cut. The state would remain poor and cut off from the rest of the nation. By 1970, 37 percent of Mississippi's population was African American. Schools were widely integrated, and a sense of racial harmony was evolving in Mississippi.

There were more changes. Farmers grew crops other than cotton and started raising livestock. Manufacturing expanded. For the first time in Mississippi history, more people worked in manufacturing trades than in farmwork. And, since 1965's Voting Rights Act, more than 250,000 black Mississippians had registered to vote.

Progress continued through the 1980s, when the state welcomed new industries and businesses. Voters elected

African Americans to many political offices. In 1990, state legislators voted in favor of opening gambling casinos along the Gulf Coast and Mississippi River. Casinos and tourism brought a huge economic benefit to the state.

Mississippi's African American population began to increase in the early 21st century. Blacks who had left were moving back. They became part of the dynamic growth and progress in their state.

Nearly all the violence of Mississippi's past has disappeared. Controversy remains over flying Mississippi's state flag, since it features a Confederate symbol that people associate with slavery. In 2001, Governor Ronnie Musgrove proposed a new design for the state flag, but so far no change has been made.

Mississippians are letting people know that things have changed. In 2006, businessman Rick Looser put $300,000 of his own money into a "Mississippi, Believe It!" advertising campaign that focuses on Mississippi's positive aspects. His efforts have attracted new businesses. Today, Mississippi is a place of great opportunity. Its people have opened their doors and their minds and welcomed progress.

A poster from the Mississippi, Believe It! campaign

66

READ ABOUT

Junior high school students make paper cranes to commemorate victims of the September II, 2OOI, terror attacks.

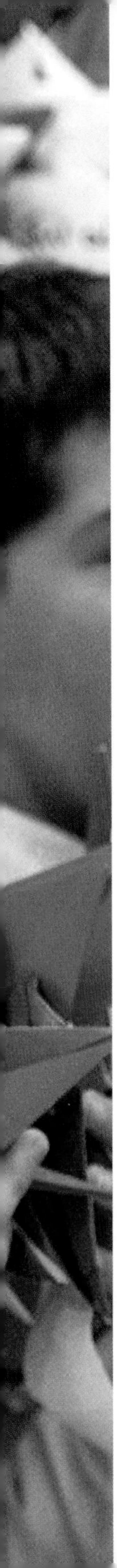

CHAPTER SIX

PEOPLE

★

M AYBE IT'S THE MILD CLIMATE, OR THE MOUTHWATERING SOUTHERN COOKING, OR THE FACT THAT MISSISSIPPI DOES NOT HAVE MANY BIG, BUSY CITIES. Whatever the reason, Mississippians mostly consider themselves laid-back, friendly people. They call their home turf the "Hospitality State," meaning they have a generous and welcoming nature.

Students on campus at the University of Southern Mississippi in Hattiesburg

Big-City Life

This list shows the population of Mississippi's biggest cities.

Jackson 176,614
Gulfport 64,316
Hattiesburg 48,012
Biloxi 44,342

Source: U.S. Census Bureau, 2006 estimate

IN THE CITY AND THE COUNTRY

Mississippi has long been a state where more people live a rural life than an urban one. But that began to change near the end of the 20th century, as more people migrated from farms and villages to larger towns and cities. Today, Mississippi's population tops out at only 2,910,540, much less than New York and Los Angeles, America's two largest cities. Of that number, 51 percent live in rural areas. A full 49 percent of Mississippians now live in towns. Most of these people live in the Jackson area and in cities along the Gulf Coast. In the coming years, however, many people believe the population will shift as casinos are built in the northwest part of the state, and with the opening of a Toyota assembly plant near Tupelo.

Jackson, the state's largest urban area, has fewer than 200,000 residents. City dwellers in Jackson, Gulfport, and Mississippi's other larger cities find that

Where Mississippians Live

The colors on this map indicate population density throughout the state. The darker the color, the more people live there.

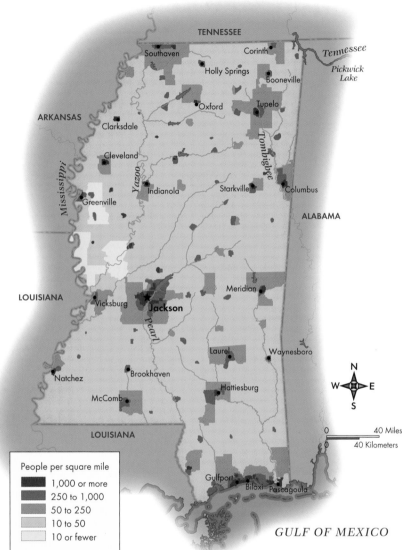

People per square mile
- 1,000 or more
- 250 to 1,000
- 50 to 250
- 10 to 50
- 10 or fewer

GULF OF MEXICO

life is not quite as frantic and stressful as it can be in big cities outside the state.

Of the Native Americans living in Mississippi, most are Choctaws who live on the Choctaw Indian Reservation in the eastern part of the state. The Asian population is made up mainly of Chinese, Vietnamese, and Filipinos. The earliest Chinese immigrants came to Mississippi as indentured servants to work on building railroads. Since Reconstruction, the greatest numbers of Chinese have lived in the Delta region. Most Vietnamese and Filipinos live along the Gulf Coast and work in the fishing industries. Hispanics live throughout the state, but are mostly in the southern

People QuickFacts

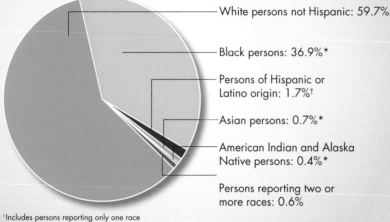

White persons not Hispanic: 59.7%

Black persons: 36.9%*

Persons of Hispanic or Latino origin: 1.7%†

Asian persons: 0.7%*

American Indian and Alaska Native persons: 0.4%*

Persons reporting two or more races: 0.6%

†Includes persons reporting only one race
*Hispanics may be of any race, so they also are included in applicable race categories
Source: U.S. Census Bureau, 2005 estimate

and western regions. The Hispanic population increased 60 percent between 1980 and 2000.

In the decades after the Civil War, many African Americans fled Mississippi. But in recent years, the black population has been increasing as many people who left the state, or their relatives, return to settle here again.

Mississippi Population Growth

This chart shows Mississippi's population growth between 1800 and 2000, and it projects that by 2010 there will be nearly 3 million people living in the state.

Source: U.S. Census Bureau

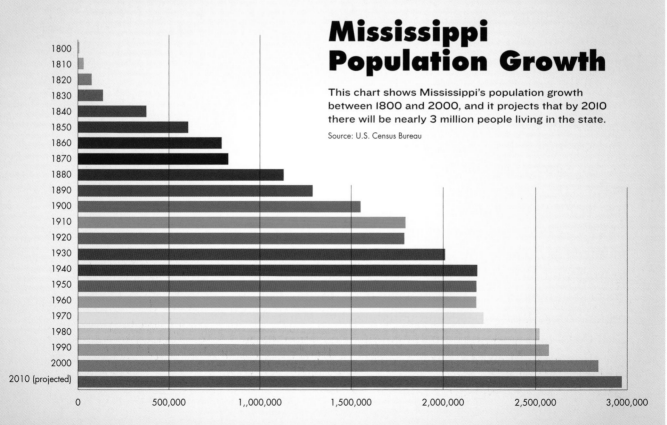

This student makes a calculation in math class. Mississippi has made great strides in improving the quality of the state's education.

STRIDES IN EDUCATION

Today, almost 74 percent of Mississippians graduate from high school (the national average is about 85 percent). Educators face many challenges. Nearly 10 percent of the population still makes it only as far as ninth grade, and the dropout rate is one of the worst in the nation. Additionally, only 17 percent of people over age 25 have college degrees. In the rest of the country, that average is 25 percent.

The state has implemented a plan to radically redesign the entire school system. The plan includes retraining teachers, buying new textbooks and other materials and equipment, developing new courses, and establishing career-focused curricula that will appeal to students. The future of higher education in the state looks much brighter.

EDUCATION FIRSTS

In 1871, Mississippi provided land and money to found Alcorn University, today the oldest land grant college in the world for black students. In 1884, the state also established Mississippi University for Women, the country's first state college for women. Mississippi was also the first state in the nation to create a junior college system.

HOW TO TALK LIKE A MISSISSIPPIAN

No matter where they live in the state, Mississippians have a few unique words in their vocabulary. Many originate in Natchez. There, a "pukah" is a big, usually wooden fan that hangs over the dining room table to keep flies off the food. A "tester" (usually pronounced "teester") is the canopy hanging over an antique bed. A "dogtrot house" is an open passageway between two rooms of the house. This area was sometimes used to pen the family pet. If you are going to take someone somewhere, you will probably "carry" him or her, as in, "I carried my grandmother to the store."

HOW TO EAT LIKE A MISSISSIPPIAN

Like other southerners, Mississippians are big on barbecue, mashed potatoes smothered in gravy, fried chicken, dumplings, pecan pie, and plenty of sweet iced tea. Mississippi's fertile farmland puts tasty fruits and vegetables such as okra, turnip greens, peaches, and sweet potatoes on the Mississippi menu.

Shrimp and many kinds of fresh fish come from the Gulf waters. Crawdads—little lobster-shaped shellfish also known as crawfish or crayfish—are harvested from the Mississippi basin. One of the state's most important catches is the catfish, which comes mainly from the Delta region. No menu of Mississippi basics would be complete without it!

Crawdad

MENU

WHAT'S ON THE MENU IN MISSISSIPPI?

★ ★ ★

Fried Dill Pickles

This delicacy comes from Hollywood, Mississippi. According to folks in the Delta region, in 1969, a young man opened the Hollywood Café and came up with this item as an appetizer. Sometimes, after they're deep-fried in batter, the pickles are sliced and eaten as chips.

Hush Puppies

These tasty bites are made by rolling a dough of cornmeal, flour, milk, egg, and a few other ingredients into balls and deep-frying them. Several tales explain how the name *hush puppies* came to be. One says that in Civil War times, Confederate troops fed the little balls to their barking dogs to hush them up when Union troops were nearby.

Okra

Tried it fried or steamed. This little vegetable is as southern as it gets!

Shrimp

The Gulf of Mexico produces loads of shrimp, and the people of Mississippi benefit! Boiled shrimp and cocktail sauce is a treat.

TRY THIS RECIPE
Sweet Potato Muffins

Mississippi farms produce lots of great food, including tasty and nutritious sweet potatoes. Here's a recipe for turning them into delicious muffins that your family and friends may enjoy. Just be sure to have a adult nearby to help.

Ingredients:
¾ cup oat bran
¾ cup whole wheat flour
⅔ cup sugar
1-½ tsp. ground cinnamon
1 tsp. baking powder
1 tsp. baking soda
pinch of salt
½ cup apples, peeled and chopped
1 cup raisins (optional)
1 cup fresh sweet potatoes, cooked and mashed
1 large egg
2 large egg whites
3 tablespoons vegetable oil
⅔ cup plain yogurt

Instructions:
Preheat oven to 350 degrees F. In a bowl, combine bran, flour, sugar, cinnamon, baking powder, baking soda, salt, and apples (and raisins if desired). Whip egg whites. In another bowl, combine sweet potatoes, egg, oil, and yogurt. Fold in egg whites. Add sweet potato mixture to flour mixture and stir together until just moistened. Spray muffin tins with cooking spray and spoon ¼ cup of batter per muffin. Bake for 25 to 30 minutes (or until a toothpick inserted in a muffin comes out clean). Makes about 20 muffins.

Sweet potato muffins

The Choctaws have a long tradition of basket making, and Mississippi artisans continue to weave baskets as their ancestors did.

ARTISTIC RICHES

Mississippi is rich in art museums, symphony halls, international ballet competitions, and theaters. Throughout Mississippi, you'll find hundreds of fascinating festivals, culturally diverse fairs, folk dancing demonstrations, and folk art museums and galleries.

Artists of all kinds are part of this cultural richness. Many are unique talents. Ethel Wright Mohamed was known as the Grandma Moses of Stitchery because she "painted with thread." Her works have been shown in the Smithsonian Institution, and many more hang in Mama's Dream World, her former home in Belzoni.

The Choctaw nation's artisans have greatly enriched Mississippi's cultural heritage, especially with beautiful basketry and beadwork. Choctaw basket weavers use the same methods and sometimes the same materials their ancestors did centuries ago. Baskets are woven from swamp cane found in Mississippi creeks. After the cane is cut into strips, it is dyed in rich shades of red, yellow, purple, brown, and black. Today, most weavers use commercial dyes, but years ago the dyes came mainly from boiled plant roots, fruits, and the bark of various trees. The end result is richly textured baskets and hampers that are treasured works of art.

Choctaw beadwork is equally stunning. Traditionally, both men and women wore various kinds of beaded decoration. One of the most common of these was the beaded sash. Today, Choctaw artisans also create collar necklaces, beaded belts, earrings, lapel pins, and much more.

Covington County, north of Hattiesburg, is the center of another of Mississippi's unique cultures. Many Old Order German Baptists have made this part of the state their home, especially Hot Coffee, Mississippi. Yep, that's the name! The German Baptists shun television, cars, and other modern conveniences. Farming is the basis of their lives, but they are also known for their beautiful basketry and patchwork quilts.

Next time you watch television or go to the movies, you might see some Mississippi natives or creations. Jim Henson, who invented Kermit the Frog, Miss Piggy, and other beloved Muppet characters for the television show *Sesame Street*, was a native of Greenville. Actor James Earl Jones was born in Arkabutla. He starred in *Field of Dreams*, and he also provided the voice of Darth

JIM HENSON: FATHER OF THE MUPPETS

Using part of a Ping-Pong ball and some fabric from his mother's old coat, Jim Henson (1936–1990) created his first famous puppet character, Kermit the Frog. Born in Greenville, Henson went on to achieve spectacular success as the "father" of the beloved Muppets.

Henson's career as a puppeteer began in high school, and by college he was performing on television. After his Muppet characters became the center of the show *Sesame Street* on public television, Henson became widely renowned. In Leland, you can visit the Birthplace of the Frog Museum, a tribute to world-famous Kermit and his Muppet friends.

? Want to know more?
See www.jimhensonlegacy.org

MINI-BIO

EUDORA WELTY: AWARD-WINNING AUTHOR

Born in Jackson, Eudora Welty (1909–2001) traveled all over the state as a photographer for the Works Progress Administration in the 1930s. No doubt, many of the people she encountered inspired the short stories and novels she became famous for. Welty's most noted short stories include "A Worn Path," "Petrified Man," and "Why I Live at the P.O." Among her best-known novels are *Delta Wedding, The Ponder Heart,* and *The Optimist's Daughter,* which earned her the 1973 Pulitzer Prize. In 1992, she received the Rea Award for the Short Story in recognition of her lifetime achievement. Welty died at age 92 and is buried at Greenwood Cemetery in her hometown.

❓ Want to know more?
See www.olemiss.edu/depts/english/
ms-writers/dir/welty_eudora/

Vader in the Star Wars movies and Mufasa in *The Lion King*. Sela Ward of Meridian is often seen on TV, and talk-show host Oprah Winfrey was born in Kosciusko.

LITERARY LIVES

Many of Mississippi's most remarkable and important contributions to the arts have been in literature. William Faulkner, Eudora Welty, Richard Wright, and Tennessee Williams are authors renowned worldwide. All

Willie Morris, seen here at his desk at *Harper's* magazine in 1971, grew up in Yazoo City and wrote the children's book *My Dog Skip*.

were Mississippi natives who described the difficult class or racial relations unique to their state's society. More current well-known authors include Willie Morris, who wrote *My Dog Skip* (which became a feature film), and Ellen Douglas, the pen name of Josephine Ayres Haxton, who has written numerous short stories and novels, including *The Rock Cried Out*.

THE SOUNDS OF MUSIC

Mississippi is the birthplace of not only many great musicians but also of one of America's great musical forms—the blues. This genre's earliest origins are in the "field hollers" of the 1800s. These were snippets of song that workers in Mississippi's cotton fields sang back and forth to one another. Soon, a distinct style of music, often sad, sometimes joyous, developed out of this "answer-back" technique. It became known as the blues.

The sound of the Mississippi Delta blues is particularly recognizable, in large part, because it often includes a slide guitar. The distinctive sound—along with the fact that so many of the greatest "bluesmen," and some fine female blues singers, too, came from the Delta—put

MINI-BIO

77

RICHARD WRIGHT: NOTED NOVELIST

Richard Wright (1908–1960) was one of the first African American writers to achieve widespread fame both in the United States and abroad. He was born on a plantation outside of Natchez. His first novel, *Native Son*, was published in 1938, and many works followed. His most acclaimed book, *Black Boy*, was released in 1945. That book, an autobiography of his younger years, painted a searing picture of racism in the American South. In 1947, Wright became a French citizen. He never returned to the United States. He died in Paris on November 28, 1960.

? **Want to know more?** See www.olemiss.edu/depts/english/ms-writers/dir/wright_richard/

SEE IT HERE!

TENNESSEE WILLIAMS WELCOME CENTER

This welcome center in Columbus was the first home of Pulitzer Prize–winning playwright Tennessee Williams. He spent his early years in this house, which was actually the rectory for St. Paul's Episcopal Church. His grandfather, Reverend Walker Dakin, served there.

In 1993, the building was in danger of being torn down when the church was expanding. Instead, it was moved to its current location on Main Street. Today, it is recognized as a national literary landmark.

this region on the music map. Robert Johnson, Muddy Waters, and B. B. King, three blues greats, all came from small towns in the Mississippi Delta region. Today, it's still one of the most rocking parts of the country!

Elvis Presley, one of the most famous musicians ever, was born in Tupelo. He was known as the King of Rock 'n' Roll for the way he transformed music in the 1950s. Many country music stars are Mississippians, including LeAnn Rimes, Faith Hill, and Jimmy Rodgers, the Father of Country Music.

Elvis Presley, born in Tupelo, was known as the King of Rock 'n' Roll.

MINI-BIO

B. B. KING: BLUES MUSICIAN

The legendary blues musician B. B. King (1925—) has received countless awards and honors, including 18 Grammys, the music industry's top honor. He has been inducted into the Rock and Roll Hall of Fame and the Blues Foundation Hall of Fame.

Born Riley B. King on a plantation in the Delta region, B. B. was the son of poor sharecroppers who separated when he was five. King managed to get a guitar and learn how to play it by reading a do-it-yourself instructional manual he had ordered through the mail. His fame and good fortune have increased as each new generation discovers his powerful and moving sound. Using his beloved Gibson guitar, Lucille, B. B. has collaborated with scores of modern blues and pop musicians.

 Want to know more? See www.bbking.com

Noted soprano Leontyne Price is from Laurel. She is seen here performing with the Boston Symphony and conductor Seiji Ozawa.

Elizabeth Taylor Greenfield, born enslaved in Natchez in 1809, was the first renowned African American classical singer. Known as the Black Swan, she wowed audiences in New York, Boston, and Chicago. She even performed for Queen Victoria in England in 1854. William Grant Still, born in 1895, was the first African American to conduct a major symphony orchestra, and his work *A Bayou Legend* was the first opera by an African American to be broadcast on national television. Leontyne Price rose from poverty in segregated Laurel, Mississippi, to become one of the greatest sopranos of all time.

SPORTS STARS

Mississippi may not have any professional sports teams, but, oh, do they love their college teams! The University of Mississippi (Ole Miss) has a powerhouse football team. The Ole Miss Rebels have dedicated fans, as do their rival Mississippi State Bulldogs. Both universities also boast solid baseball and basketball teams.

History-Making Coach

If you watch college or professional football, you'll marvel at the talented athletes from all kinds of backgrounds. But you might notice that there aren't that many African American coaches. In fact, until 2003, there were no African American head coaches in the Southeastern Conference college football programs. All that changed when Sylvester Croom was named head football coach at Mississippi State University (MSU). Buck Showalter, who used to play baseball at MSU before his professional career, said: "I don't think there is a prouder moment for my school. I'm proud that my school has the vision to do the right thing. It's long overdue. He deserves the job. It's tough these days to have an ethical and a winning program at the same time, a program that alumni can be proud of."

Other athletes who hail from Mississippi include Brett Favre, quarterback for the Green Bay Packers, who was born in Gulfport and played football at the University of Southern Mississippi. Steve McNair, quarterback for the Tennessee Titans, was born in Mount Olive and played for Alcorn State University near Loman. Jerry Rice, born in Crawford and considered one of the greatest wide receivers in NFL history, won three Super Bowl rings with the San Francisco 49ers. Walter Payton, who was born in Columbia, played for Jackson State University and went on to be a running back for the Chicago Bears.

Baseball history has roots in Mississippi. Cool Papa Bell, a center fielder in the Negro Leagues, was born in Starkville. Dizzy Dean was a legendary pitcher with the St. Louis Cardinals and Chicago Cubs. He was a resident of Wiggins, Mississippi.

Ruthie Bolton is a former professional basketball player from Lucedale. She played in the WNBA and won two gold medals (in 1996 and 2000) on the U.S. Olympic team. Ralph Boston was a track star from Laurel. He won a gold medal at the 1960 Olympic Games.

Mississippi is a culturally rich state that has produced great writers, educators, artists, musicians, and athletes. Their contributions help make the state unique.

Fans enjoy celebrating an Ole Miss basketball victory over Alabama in February 2007.

JERRY RICE: STAR WIDE RECEIVER

Born in Crawford, Jerry Rice (1962–) was a star on the Mississippi Valley State University football team. As a wide receiver, he set college records, including the NCAA record for most receptions in a single game: 24.

In 1985, Rice was drafted by the San Francisco 49ers. In 1988, he helped that team win the Super Bowl, with 11 receptions for 215 yards and one touchdown. He was named the Super Bowl MVP. He won two more Super Bowl rings with the 49ers in 1989 and 1994. And in 1995, he set an NFL season record, with 1,848 receiving yards for 15 touchdowns. Rice retired from the game in 2006. His total receiving yards (22,895) is just one of the many NFL records he still holds.

? Want to know more? See http://www.jerryrice football.com/

READ ABOUT

These participants in the Mississippi Youth and Government Program learn about the process of proposing and passing laws in the state.

CHAPTER SEVEN

GOVERNMENT

★

MISSISSIPPI'S STUDENTS OF TODAY WILL BE TOMORROW'S LAWMAKERS. Many young people in Jackson are already getting a taste of what governing is like. A YMCA program called the Youth and Government Program for Mississippi gives junior high students the experience of proposing, writing, and passing laws. By role-playing as members of Congress right in capitol chambers, they learn firsthand the processes and procedures that take a proposed law from idea to reality.

FAQ

Q: WHO IS THE CAPITAL CITY OF JACKSON NAMED AFTER?

A: The city's name is a tribute to Andrew Jackson, who was a war hero in Mississippi. Jackson led successful battles against British and Native American troops. Jackson later became the seventh president of the United States.

WHERE IT ALL HAPPENS

In the early 1790s, a French Canadian trader by the name of Louis LeFleur found a scenic place to settle on the banks of the Pearl River. His trading post prospered there, and the spot came to be called LeFleur's Bluff. Today, that magnolia-scented piece of land is a state park in the heart of Mississippi's capital city, Jackson.

Jackson has served as the state capital since 1822 and is a vibrant modern city. As the seat of government, it has a long and interesting past, including three different state constitutions, as well as three different capitols. The last constitution, still in use today, was approved in 1890.

The capitol in Jackson

Capital City

This map shows places of interest around Jackson, Mississippi's capital city.

JACKSON

Farish Street Historical District

Mississippi State Capitol

Galloway House

Virden-Patton House

Smith Robertson Museum and Cultural Center

Morris House

Alamo Theatre

The Mississippi Arts Center

War Memorial Building

Old Mississippi State Capitol

City Hall

International Museum of Muslim Cultures

Mississippi Governor's Mansion

Pearl River

N W E S

The first capitol was a simple brick structure. That was replaced with an elegant, Greek Revival–style building in 1839. Today, that building, the historic site at which Mississippi's legislators voted to secede from the Union, is known as the Old Capitol. The new capitol, modeled after the U.S. Capitol in Washington, D.C., has been in use since 1903. Before that, a state penitentiary stood on the same spot!

FAQ

Q8 WHAT HAPPENED TO THE OLD CAPITOL?

A8 The beautiful building is still standing and has long served as the home of the Museum of Mississippi History. The Old Capitol suffered a disaster in 2005, when Hurricane Katrina ripped into the roof of the building. Besides structural damage, wind and rain damaged some 3,200 historical artifacts, forcing the museum to close down for the time being.

WOW

The eagle that sits atop the capitol dome is a whopping 8 feet (2.4 m) tall. Its outstretched wings measure 15 feet (4.6 m) from tip to tip!

Capitol Facts

Here are some interesting facts about Mississippi's state capitol.

Building length . . . . 402 feet (122.5 m)
Exterior height to top of dome . .180 feet (55 m)
Location: . . . . .400 High Street
Years of construction 1901–1903
Cost of construction . . . . . . $1,093,641, paid for by the Illinois Central Railroad, which owed Mississippi back taxes

MINI-BIO

DAVID HOLMES: FIRST GOVERNOR OF MISSISSIPPI

David Holmes (1769–1832) was Mississippi's first governor, as well as its fifth. Before Mississippi became a state in 1817, he was the fourth governor of Mississippi Territory.

Holmes was born in Pennsylvania, but grew up in Virginia. At the time he was appointed governor of Mississippi Territory, he was a member of the U.S. Congress representing Virginia. During his first term (1817–1820), Holmes directed the creation of the state's military forces and judicial system. After this term, he was elected to the U.S. Senate and served there from 1820 to 1825. He was reelected as Mississippi governor in 1825. Holmes retired to his boyhood state of Virginia, where he died at Jordan's Sulphur Springs on August 28, 1832.

? **Want to know more?** See http://mshistory.k12.ms.us/features/feature47/governors/1_holmes.htm

SEAT OF GOVERNMENT

Mississippi's government is structured a lot like that of the federal government. The state government has three main branches: the executive, the judicial, and the legislative. All three branches of the Mississippi government were once housed in the new capitol building on High Street. Today, only the executive and legislative branches reside there. The judicial branch has its headquarters in the Gartin Justice Building, not far from the capitol.

Lieutenant Governor Amy Tuck addressing the Mississippi Economic Council in 2005

Mississippi State Government

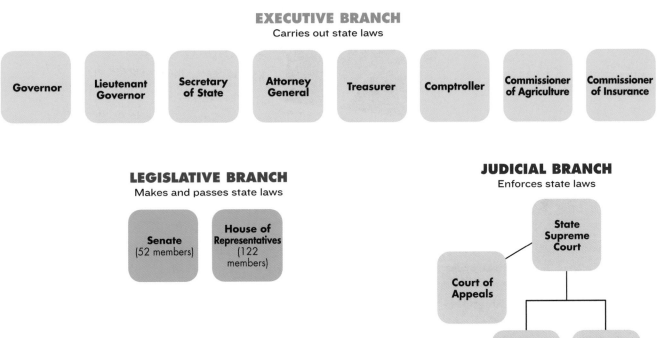

EXECUTIVE BRANCH
Carries out state laws

Governor | Lieutenant Governor | Secretary of State | Attorney General | Treasurer | Comptroller | Commissioner of Agriculture | Commissioner of Insurance

LEGISLATIVE BRANCH
Makes and passes state laws

Senate (52 members) | House of Representatives (122 members)

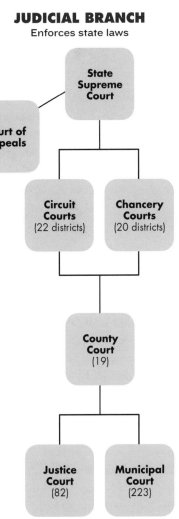

JUDICIAL BRANCH
Enforces state laws

State Supreme Court

Court of Appeals

Circuit Courts (22 districts) | Chancery Courts (20 districts)

County Court (19)

Justice Court (82) | Municipal Court (223)

THE EXECUTIVE BRANCH

The governor of Mississippi is the head of the executive branch and is elected by the people. The governor is the chief executive officer of the state, just as the president is the chief executive of the country.

The governor has many duties, such as overseeing the general administration of state business, deciding who is appointed to many different official positions within the government, and signing or vetoing laws that are passed by the legislative branch. The lieutenant governor presides over the state senate. Along with the speaker of the house, these two position wield more power than the governor, as they control committee appointments and legislative agendas. The executive branch also makes sure the state's laws are enforced.

EVELYN GANDY: LIEUTENANT GOVERNOR

Evelyn Gandy (1920–) has a long list of firsts in Mississippi politics. Born in Hattiesburg, she entered law school at the University of Mississippi in 1943, the only woman in her class. During law school, she became the first woman elected as president of the student body, as well as the first woman to edit the *Mississippi Law Journal*.

After opening her own law practice, she was elected to Mississippi's state legislature, again the first woman to hold the job. In 1959, she became both the first female assistant attorney general of Mississippi and the first female state treasurer. She went on to become Mississippi's first female state insurance commissioner in 1972, and in 1975 was elected the state's first female lieutenant governor. In 1979, she lost the race for governor by a close margin. Gandy has spent her career working tirelessly for progressive reforms, especially women's rights.

? Want to know more? See www.stennis.gov/gandy.htm

SEE IT HERE!

THE GOVERNOR'S MANSION

For a trip back in time, take a tour of Mississippi's elegant Greek Revival–style governor's mansion. Since 1842, a long line of Mississippi governors and their families have lived in the house, making it the second-oldest continuously occupied governor's mansion in the United States.

Evidence indicates that Union officers used the building at least once during the Civil War. The historic part of the mansion is open to the public, and many of the rooms have colorful names. Had you been a long-ago guest of one of Mississippi's governors, you might have slept in the Gold Bedroom, the Green Bedroom, the Cream Bedroom, or maybe even the Pumpkin Bedroom!

THE LEGISLATIVE BRANCH

The people who make the laws belong to the legislative branch. The two arms of the Mississippi legislature are the senate and the house of representatives. If the governor vetoes a bill, this branch has the power to override that veto by a two-thirds majority.

The head of the senate is the lieutenant governor. To be qualified to run for lieutenant governor, a person must have been a U.S. citizen for at least 20 years and a citizen of Mississippi for five years. He or she can be no younger than 30 years old.

To be a senator, one must be a U.S. citizen who has lived in Mississippi for at least four years and for two years in the district he or she represents. A candidate for senator must also be at least 25 years old.

Like state senators, members of the Mississippi house of representatives serve four-year terms, but they can run for office at the age of 21. Representatives must have lived in the state for a minimum of four years and in their counties for at least two years.

The senate and house of representatives are usually in session for a total of 90 days, or three months, of the year. Every four years, members of the state legislature extend their sessions to 120 days. During each session, the lawmakers may pass 500 bills or more. From there, the bills go to the governor, who either signs them to make the

ROBERT G. CLARK: MISSISSIPPI CONGRESSMAN

Robert George Clark (1928–) was the first African American to be elected to the Mississippi House of Representatives since Reconstruction. Clark was born in Ebenezer and grew up on a farm that his great-grandfather, a former slave, had bought. In college at Jackson State University, Clark majored in education, and, after graduating, he became a teacher. He also worked as a football coach. During the violent struggle for racial integration in the 1960s, he was an energetic civil rights leader. In 1968, he was elected to his first term as a Mississippi state congressman. He went on to serve several terms. In the house of representatives, he spent many years working to pass the Education Reform Act of 1982, which called for improvements throughout the state.

? Want to know more? See http://www.usm.edu/crdp/html/transcripts/manuscript-clark_robert_g.shtml

Representing Mississippi

This list shows the number of elected officials who represent Mississippi, both on the state and national levels.

OFFICE	NUMBER	LENGTH OF TERM
State senators	52	4 years
State representatives	122	4 years
U.S. senators	2	6 years
U.S. representatives	4	2 years
Presidential electors	6	—

MINI-BIO

BLANCHE K. BRUCE: U.S. SENATOR

Blanche K. Bruce (1841–1898), who escaped slavery in Virginia in 1863, studied at Oberlin College in Ohio and organized a school for former slaves. After the Civil War, he settled in Mississippi and served as a sheriff, tax collector, and school superintendent.

Bruce owned an 800-acre (324 ha) plantation and made a lot of political friends. In 1874, the state legislature elected him to the U.S. Senate. He served a full six-year term, the only black man in the 19th century to do so. He championed the right of people to live free of discrimination and violence. Bruce bravely took unpopular stands. He dared to tell his Senate colleagues that Chinese immigrants should be allowed into this country. He even publicly declared that U.S government policy toward Native Americans was unfair. No other African American would serve in the Senate until Senator Edward Brooke of Massachusetts, in 1966.

? Want to know more? See http://www.senate.gov/artandhistory/history/minute/Former_Slave_Presides_Over_Senate.htm

new laws official or vetoes them to prevent them from becoming law.

THE JUDICIAL BRANCH

The judicial branch is in charge of the courts. It makes sure there is a balance of power among all three branches of the government. The courts make rulings on whether or not executive policies are fair and legal. They also rule on whether laws passed by the legislature are constitutional or not.

The judicial branch is made up of many different courts. The most powerful of these is the state supreme court, which includes nine judges elected by the people. There are also the court of appeals, the circuit courts, county courts, and the chancery. Mississippi's chancery courts mainly handle domestic and family matters and rarely use juries.

The office of the attorney general is another important part of the judicial branch of government. The attorney general is the chief legal adviser for the state. If the state brings a lawsuit or is sued, the attorney general will handle these cases.

Mississippi Speaker of the House Billy McCoy speaks to a group of citizens about health legislation in May 2004.

LOCAL GOVERNMENT

Lawmakers in Jackson handle matters that affect the entire state. But local government is important, too. Of Mississippi's 82 counties, 72 have county seats, and each is the hub of local county business. The other 10 counties share two county seats among them. A little more than half of Mississippi's towns have local city governments.

The counties have both elected and appointed officials. A few of the elected officials include sheriffs, county prosecuting attorneys, county court judges, the superintendent of education, and the board of supervisors. Two jobs given by appointment are the justice court clerks, who keep track of lawsuits and other court business, and the county comptroller, a bookkeeper who watches over county expenses.

By tradition, on the first day of each legislative session, the capitol is all lit up—literally. For the occasion, every light on every floor is turned on—a total of 4,700 lightbulbs!

Mississippi Counties

This map shows the 82 counties in Mississippi. Jackson, the state capital, is indicated with a star.

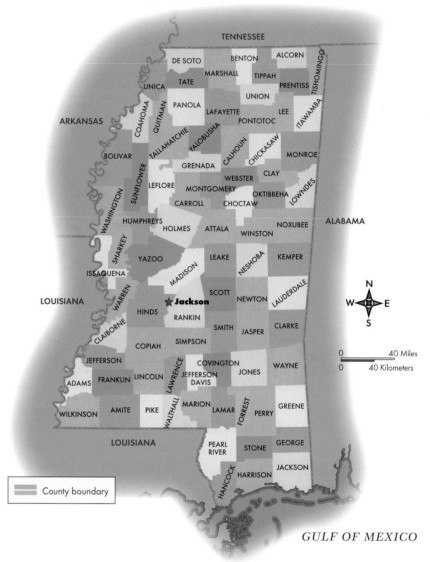

TENNESSEE

ARKANSAS

LOUISIANA

ALABAMA

★ Jackson

N
W   E
S

0   40 Miles
0   40 Kilometers

County boundary

LOUISIANA

GULF OF MEXICO

THE ROLE OF YOUNG PEOPLE

Mississippi students have had a major impact on an important issue: smoking. A 1999 survey showed that 42 percent of Mississippi's high school and junior high school students smoked or chewed tobacco. Some of them decided to do something about that, and their efforts paid off quickly. In January 2000, a student anti-

Senator Stacy Pickering speaks with a group of students participating in Lobbypalooza, an annual program sponsored by the Partnership for a Healthy Mississippi.

tobacco advocacy group known as Frontline staged a "Lobbypalooza" on the steps of the state capitol. The aim of the gathering was to get the attention of Mississippi legislators. Frontline's students, ranging from grades 8 through 12, wanted the government to pass legislation banning cigarettes, as well as chewing tobacco, from schools throughout the state.

After an intensive campaign, which included letter writing, a statewide student petition, and testimony at the state house of representatives, the students got what they wanted. In May 2000, the legislature passed House Bill 641, making it illegal for students and teachers to smoke or chew tobacco in all Mississippi schools. This includes in campus buildings, as well as on school grounds, on sports fields, and in recreational areas. It even outlaws the use of tobacco at school-sponsored off-campus events.

Mississippi's government has brought many changes to the state. One thing is for sure: Mississippi government officials will continue to work hard to maintain the state's political, social, and economic growth for years to come.

State Flag

The flag of Mississippi was designed by the state legislature and approved on February 7, 1894. The Confederate battle flag design in the upper left corner of the flag represents the state's membership in the Confederacy and demonstrates the state's strong links to the past. The Confederate battle flag was used during the Civil War. Civil rights groups have asked that the flag be changed. They believe the Confederate portion of the flag is an insult to African Americans. So far, efforts to change the flag have been unsuccessful. The remainder of the flag is made up of three horizontal bars, in the national colors of red, white, and blue.

The pledge to the state flag reads, "I salute the flag of Mississippi and the sovereign state for which it stands with pride in her history and achievements and with confidence in her future under the guidance of Almighty God." The state motto, *Virtute et Armis*, means "By Valor and Arms."

State Seal

The Mississippi state seal is very similar to the U.S. seal. At the outer perimeter of the crest are the words, "The Great Seal of the State of Mississippi." At the center of the seal stands an American eagle clasping an olive branch (the symbol of peace) and a quiver of arrows (representing the power to wage war), with a bunting of stars and stripes on its chest.

READ ABOUT

Harvesting cotton

ECONOMY ECONOMY ECONOMY ECONOMY ECONOMY ECONOMY

CHAPTER EIGHT

ECONOMY

★

W HAT DO MISSISSIPPIANS DO WHEN THEY GO OFF TO WORK? They are teachers and doctors, store clerks and businesspeople. But agriculture is still the number-one industry in the state. Only 3.4 percent of Mississippi's workforce is directly involved in agriculture, but in one way or another, a full 30 percent of the workforce works in agriculture-related industries. Farm industries pull in about $6.5 billion a year. Their work, directly or indirectly, ensures that Mississippi's farm products get to market.

Major Agricultural and Mining Products

This map shows where Mississippi's major agricultural and mining products come from. See a chicken? That means poultry is raised there.

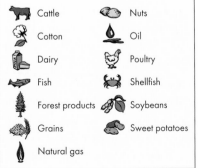

Cattle	Nuts
Cotton	Oil
Dairy	Poultry
Fish	Shellfish
Forest products	Soybeans
Grains	Sweet potatoes
Natural gas	

Legend (map):
- Urban area
- Farming
- Forests, some farming
- Grazing, rangeland
- Swampland, some farming

FARM INDUSTRIES

The biggest moneymaker in Mississippi's agricultural industry today is the poultry business. About 827 million 5-pound (2 kg) chickens, called broilers, are sold annually. Broilers and eggs bring in more than $2 billion a year!

Mississippi is a national leader in the forestry business, since dense woods still cover much of the state. It also has more tree farms than any other state. A total of 61 percent of the land goes to tree farms and harvesting timber for hundreds of commercial uses. These products bring in another $1.27 billion a year.

Cotton remains an important crop to the state, but as a $510 million industry, it's fairly far behind the other two leaders. Nevertheless, Mississippi is the nation's third-largest cotton producer.

All those hens at Mississippi's poultry farms produce 1.6 billion eggs a year!

FOOD FROM THE WATERS

Nobody can travel through Mississippi without hearing about, and probably tasting, one of the state's biggest income-producing foods. That's catfish. Catfish are scavengers. That means they go trawling along the bottoms of lakes and streams looking for whatever they can find to eat. As a result, a lot of people didn't like the taste of this big fish.

A haul of catfish from the Mississippi Delta

Today, farm-raised catfish are bred to have a mild, nonfishy taste. As a result, the demand for this fish has grown tremendously. Once, it was just a Southern specialty. Now, people all across the country and around the world are discovering how good catfish is, thanks mainly to the catfish farms that stretch across the Mississippi Delta region. Thirty-two percent of the nation's commercial farm-raised catfish comes from here, making it the state's fourth-largest agricultural product. It's a $274 million business!

Shrimp fishing in the Gulf of Mexico makes Mississippi a leader in that industry, too. But compared to catfish farming, shrimping is a slightly "shrimpy" business.

FACTORIES

Modern Mississippi has several highly successful manufacturing industries. Products made in the state are exported to more than 100 countries around the world.

Mississippi is the nation's leading manufacturer of upholstered furniture. Food processing, factories that produce transportation and electrical equipment, and the production of chemicals and pharmaceuticals are other top-producing industries. Dozens of other products are manufactured here, as well.

Recently, another Mississippi industry has been seeing rapid growth. During World War II, shipbuilding was a big business in the Gulf Coast. After the war, that activity all but died away. Today, shipbuilding is back. With access to both the Gulf of Mexico and the Mississippi River, the state has a lot to offer shipbuilders, and in

Top Products

Agriculture Poultry and eggs, forestry, cotton, soybeans, catfish, cattle, rice, corn, hay, horticulture

Manufacturing Shipbuilding, furniture manufacturing, food processing, industrial chemicals and drug manufacturing

Mining Petroleum (oil), natural gas, mineral products

recent years, many have relocated here. Besides vessels that carry goods, Mississippi's shipyards produce nuclear-powered submarines and other ships for the U.S. Navy.

MINING

Mineral products, natural gas liquids, and crude petroleum have become important products in Mississippi. Only 12 states produce more of these products, which are mined both on land and using offshore oil rigs in the Gulf. Other products, such as sand, limestone, gravel, and clay, account for only 10 percent of the state's mining activities.

SERVICE INDUSTRIES

Just like in any other state, Mississippi relies heavily on its service industries. These are things such as health care, hotels and motels, restaurants, and shops and businesses of all kinds. Service industries provide more jobs for Mississippians than any other industry.

One service industry has recently exploded onto the scene—gambling casinos. In a

The "Gorilla," built in Vicksburg, is a mobile offshore oil rig. It is the world's biggest rig of its kind. The Gorilla measures 600 feet (183 m) tall and weighs a massive 38 million pounds (17.3 million kg)!

MINI-BIO

PHILLIP MARTIN: CHOCTAW BUSINESSMAN

Chief Phillip Martin (1926–) is one of the leading businessmen in the state of Mississippi. He has also done more for the advancement of the 8,300 Mississippi Choctaws than any other single individual. He was named Citizen of the Year for Philadelphia (Mississippi) and Neshoba County in 1997, and in 1999 he was elected to his sixth consecutive six-year term as chief of the Mississippi band.

As chief, Martin has established many profitable businesses, bringing hundreds of millions of dollars to the 30,000-acre (12,100 ha) Choctaw reservation in eastern Mississippi. Two of the most profitable of these have been high-end gaming casinos and golf courses. Under Martin's direction, the Choctaw tribe has become the largest employer in eastern Mississippi and the third-largest in the state. In the 1970s, Choctaw unemployment was at 75 percent. Today, it stands at only about 6 percent.

? **Want to know more?** See www.choctaw.org/government/office_of_the_chief.htm

few years, a total of 27 casinos have opened in Mississippi. Most of them are located in counties along the Gulf Coast and the Mississippi River. The casino business has grown so rapidly that Mississippi is now the number two gaming state, outdone only by Nevada. Together, Mississippi's casinos provide thousands of jobs.

What Do Mississippians Do?

This color-coded chart shows what industries Mississippians work in.

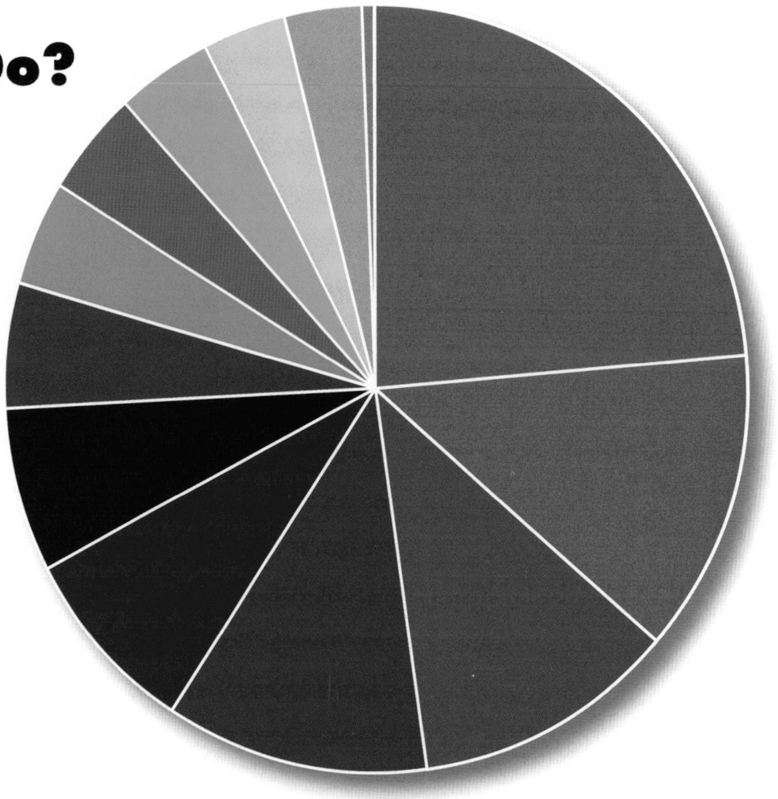

23.7% Educational, health, and social services, 750,610

12.8% Manufacturing, 405,368

11.6% Professional, scientific, management, administrative, and waste management services, 365,561

11.2% Retail trade, 353,019

8.2% Finance, insurance, real estate, and rental and leasing, 259,538

6.8% Arts, entertainment, recreation, accommodation and food services, 214,026

5.5% Construction, 173,940

4.4% Other services (except public administration), 138,635

4.3% Public administration, 134,365

4.2% Transportation and warehousing, and utilities, 131,820

3.7% Information, 118,432

3.3% Wholesale trade, 103,333

0.4% Agriculture, forestry, fishing and hunting, and mining, 12,440

Source: U.S. Census Bureau, 2000

AEROSPACE INDUSTRY

If you want to go to the moon, you have to go through Hancock County, Mississippi. At least that's what they used to say at the John C. Stennis Space Center (SSC), which is located there. That's because the Apollo space program, which successfully sent the first astronauts to the moon in the late 1960s, never could have happened without the work done at the SSC. Before the Apollo vehicle and its astronauts ever left the ground, its engines were carefully tested for safety at the SSC.

In fact, this remarkable facility is where the National Aeronautics and Space Administration (NASA) tests most of its rocket engines. The center, which is named for Senator John C. Stennis, a strong supporter of NASA, has more than 30 different agencies, which altogether employ more than 5,000 people. Being home to the SSC has made Mississippi an important part of NASA's space program since the 1960s.

LOOKING TO THE FUTURE

In Mississippi, the seven fastest-growing jobs are now related to the service industry, especially medical fields. The need for medical assistants, physical therapists, and biomedical engineers is on the rise. The highest salaries come from jobs in company management, utilities, mining, and professional and technical services.

Once, Mississippians may have voluntarily chosen to isolate themselves from what was happening in the wider world. But now, Mississippi faces global demands for its products. The state is welcoming new opportunities of all kinds, and it's taking steps to attract people from out of state, both as tourists and new business associates. Industries that once had little impact on the state are growing rapidly.

SEE IT HERE!

THE SSC STENNISSPHERE

The Stennis Space Center is not just a place for on-the-job scientists. It is *the* place in Mississippi for future scientists, future astronauts, and anyone interested in the wide world of space. Not surprisingly, a visit to the StennisSphere, the facility's visitor center, begins at the Launch Pad. From there, you'll experience an exciting interactive trip into the nation's largest rocket engine test facility. As well as checking out real rocket engines, you can take a walk under the sea, explore a module of an international space station, and climb inside the cockpit of a space shuttle replica.

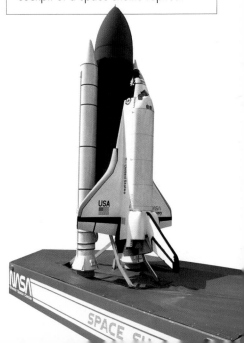

TENNESSEE

Tennessee

Pickwick Lake

Southaven
Olive Branch
Corinth
Iuka

Hollywood
Holly Springs
Booneville

Tunica
Arkabutla
Tishomingo

Sledge
Oxford
Tupelo
Fulton

ARKANSAS

Clarksdale
Coffeeville
Okolona

Rosedale
Grenada
Egypt
West Point

Cleveland
Tombighee

Benoit
Greenwood
Starkville
Columbus

Shaw
Indianola
Crawford

Greenville
Belzoni
Natchez Trace Pkwy.

Yazoo City
Kosciusko
Geographic Center of Mississippi
Choctaw

N
W ✦ **E**
S

0   40 Miles
0   40 Kilometers

Mississippi

Yazoo

55

Canton
Carthage
Philadelphia

Madison
Decatur

Ridgeland
ALABAMA

Vicksburg
Clinton
Brandon
20
Meridian

LOUISIANA
Pearl
Jackson

Utica
Pearl

Port Gibson
Hot Coffee
Laurel

Lorman
Collins
Waynesboro

Fayette
59

Washington
Brookhaven
Hattiesburg

Natchez

McComb
Columbia

Woodville
Lucedale

LOUISIANA

| **20** | Interstate highway |

Picayune
Ocean Springs
Gulfport

12
Long Beach

10

Bay St. Louis
Biloxi
Pascagoula

GULF OF MEXICO

10

CHAPTER NINE

TRAVEL GUIDE

★

Have you ever thought about visiting the birthplace of the king of rock 'n' roll or walking the land where some of the most dramatic events of the civil rights movement took place? Ever imagined exploring the site of a Civil War battle? How about experiencing a Native American dance ceremony or witnessing a fleet of shrimp boats being blessed? You can do all of this in Mississippi—and much more.

← Follow along with this travel map. We'll begin in Corinth and travel all the way south to Bay Saint Louis!

HILLS REGION

THINGS TO DO: Visit historic sites, learn about the blues, see some great cars, and tour the home of a rock 'n' roll legend.

Corinth

★ **Corinth Freedman's Camp:** During the Civil War, this secret Union army encampment hid escaping slaves.

★ **Civil War Earthworks:** Recognized as a national historic landmark, this earthworks system of fortifications was built in Corinth by Union and Confederate armies during the Civil War.

★ **Black History Museum of Corinth:** This museum is run by volunteers, and it features artifacts and memorabilia related to the history and contributions of African Americans in Corinth.

Black History Museum of Corinth

SEE IT HERE!

CIVIL WAR REENACTMENT

Go back in time and experience the Civil War era for yourself. This reenactment in Grenada, which occurs each September, features men dressed in uniforms as Union and Confederate soldiers. You'll also see Confederate camps, smoking cannons, women in hoopskirts, and a political rally. There's also a ghost walk that takes visitors to historic spots around town.

Grenada

★ **Grenada Confederate Forts:** These field fortifications were set up by Confederate forces as protection from General U. S. Grant and the approaching Union army.

Oxford

★ **Center for the Study of Southern Culture:** Part of the University of Mississippi, this center is focused on sharing and interpreting the story of the American South.

★ **Rowan Oak:** Author William Faulkner bought this 1848 Greek Revival house in 1930, and for the rest of his life, he worked to restore and pay for it. More than 20,000 visitors come each year to see where Faulkner wrote his novels.

SEE IT HERE!

ELVIS PRESLEY BIRTHPLACE AND MUSEUM

In Tupelo, you'll find the birthplace of Elvis Presley. The home was built in 1934 by Elvis's father, and the museum houses a collection of Elvis memorabilia. Every August, fans gather to remember the birth of the king of rock 'n' roll. A driving tour highlights the important places in Elvis's early life. Come see where it all began!

Elvis Presley Birthplace and Museum

★ **University of Mississippi:** Ole Miss opened its doors to 80 students in 1848. Today, its enrollment totals about 17,300 students. Its main library houses the Hall of Mississippi Writers and the Music and Blues Archive, among other important collections.

Holly Springs

★ **Ida B. Wells-Barnett Museum:** The well-preserved home that houses this museum was built before the Civil War. It is the birthplace of Ida B. Wells-Barnett, one of Mississippi's most important civil rights workers. Inside you'll find a great collection of family heirlooms, as well as many artifacts of African American heritage and culture.

Tupelo

★ **Tupelo Auto Museum:** If you like old cars, this is the place to go. The museum's $6 million collection includes 150 amazing old cars and also an 1886 motorized carriage that some call the world's first automobile.

DELTA REGION

THINGS TO DO: Listen to great music, visit plantations, and get a look at Civil War landmarks.

Clarksdale

★ **Delta Blues Museum:** This place has the biggest collection of blues artifacts and memorabilia you might ever come across—including the cabin where Muddy Waters, a legendary blues musician, grew up!

Music legend Paul Simon (left) with South African musician Joseph Shambalala, of Ladysmith Black Mambazo, at the Delta Blues Museum

Greenville

★ **Winterville Mounds and Museum:** This is the site of a prehistoric ceremonial center built by a Native American civilization that thrived from about 1000 CE to 1450. The mounds, part of the Winterville society's religious system, were the site of sacred structures and ceremonies.

★ **The Great Wall of Mississippi:** In 1927, rising river waters put so much pressure on the levee north of Greenville that it broke, and thousands of acres were flooded. When this new levee was built, it was meant to last.

The Great Wall of Mississippi is taller than the Great Wall of China—and you can walk along the top of it!

Greenwood

★ **Fort Pemberton Civil War Site:** Imagine the sights and sounds of the Civil War as you tour this historic landmark.

★ **Greenwood Blues Heritage Museum and Gallery:** Learn about Greenwood's role in blues music in this museum containing the foremost collection of recordings and memorabilia related to Delta guitarist Robert Johnson.

Indianola

★ **The B. B. King Museum and Delta Interpretive Center:** This museum began in 2005 to commemorate the life and music of B. B. King. Visitors walk through the brick cotton gin building where the young King once worked. Inside, try mixing your own music in a real studio!

Tunica

★ **Tunica RiverPark:** No trip to the Delta would be complete without a visit to this eco-park. It's the place to explore and understand the mighty Mississippi River. The RiverPark Museum and Aquarium features an interactive center where you'll get an underwater view of a swamp and learn about the region's Native Americans, the European explorers, and the great flood of 1927. Outside, walk trails, watch the river from the observation deck, or ride on a classic 1800s riverboat.

Tunica RiverPark

PINES REGION

THINGS TO DO: Hike through an incredible forest, learn about a country music legend, and check out carousel horses on display.

Choctaw

★ **Choctaw Museum of the Southern Indian:** Learn about Choctaw traditions and their arts and crafts through exhibits, photos, and videos. The museum is located on the Choctaw Indian Reservation.

Meridian

★ **Lazy Acres Plantation:** Come in October and you'll find plenty to do in this giant pumpkin patch. Get lost trying to find your way out of the corn maze, chill out on a hayride, or go hog wild watching the pig races.

★ **Jimmie Rodgers Museum:** Fashioned after an old train depot, this museum houses souvenirs and memorabilia of the "Father of Country Music," including a rare Martin 00045 guitar!

Philadelphia

★ **Nanih Waiya Mound and Village Historic Site:** The site plays a central role in the Choctaw tribe's origin legends. In one version, the mound gave birth to the tribe—the people emerged from the underworld here and rested on the mound's slopes to dry before populating the surrounding region.

★ **Williams Brothers Store:** This historic general store was founded in 1907 and still retains its old-style charm. You can buy feed and seed, wheels of cheese, shoes, blue jeans, and much more.

Starkville

★ **Aspen Bay Candle Company Factory:** The Aspen Bay Candle Company produces and manufactures some of the best-smelling and best-selling candles around!

SEE IT HERE!

TOMBIGBEE NATIONAL FOREST

Be sure to take a day or two and visit this beautiful 66,600-acre (26,950 ha) national forest, located in Chickasaw County. There are lots of activities, including hiking, boating, and camping. You can go for a swim in Davis Lake or a horseback ride on the 18-mile (29 km) loop.

Kosciusko

★ **L. V. Hull's Ethnic Yard Art:**
Walk through this wonderland of
used everyday items, from tele-
phones and paintbrushes to baskets
and car tires, collected into one big
art piece!

Columbus

★ **Friendship Cemetery:** Veterans of
wars dating back to the American
Revolution lie here, including five
Confederate generals and scores
of Civil War soldiers. Each spring,
visitors watch as costumed actors
portray some of the famous figures
buried here.

CAPITAL/ RIVER REGION

**THINGS TO DO: Examine the
life of a literary genius, visit museums, and
find out about Native American history.**

Jackson

★ **Eudora Welty House:** Visit the
home that celebrates the life of
Pulitzer Prize winner Eudora
Welty. She spent most of her
life in Jackson and is buried in
Greenwood Cemetery.

★ **Mississippi Agriculture and
Forestry/National Agricultural
Aviation Museum:** Discover
Mississippi's proud agricultural
legacy as your guide explains how
agriculture and forestry molded the
history and heritage of the state.

FAQ ★ ∴

Q8 WHY IS FRIENDSHIP CEMETERY SO FAMOUS?

A8 Besides its many famous dead and scores
of unmarked graves, the cemetery is well-known
for another reason. On April 25, 1866, four
Columbus women brought armloads of fresh
flowers to the cemetery and laid them on the
graves of soldiers, Union and Confederate alike.
This turned into an annual celebration known as
Decoration Day, which is said to be the origin of
our modern Memorial Day.

Mississippi Agriculture Museum

SEE IT HERE!

MISSISSIPPI MUSEUM OF NATURAL SCIENCE

This interactive museum in Jackson explores Mississippi's biological diversity. Check out the 100,000-gallon (400,000 liter) aquarium system that contains more than 200 species of native fishes, reptiles, amphibians, and other creatures. The 1,700-square-foot (160 sq m) greenhouse is home to alligators, turtles, and a lush native plant garden. Enjoy more than 2.5 miles (4 km) of walking trails that wind through the 300-acre (120 ha) outdoor area.

Want to know more? See www.mdwfp.com/museum/default.asp

Parts of the Natchez Trace Parkway run through cypress swamps.

★ **Mississippi Museum of Art:** This museum's permanent collection is three-quarters American art and features works by Albert Bierstadt, Georgia O'Keeffe, James Whistler, and many others. The collection also includes works by Mississippi natives, as well as European, Asian, and ethnographic art.

Clay image from the Mississippi Museum of Art

Natchez

★ **Natchez Trace Parkway:** One of the South's most historic roads begins here and extends 444 miles (715 km) nearly all the way to Nashville, Tennessee. The parkway follows the ancient Natchez Trace, an 8,000-year-old path through the wilderness that took Native Americans, explorers, settlers, and adventurers from one end of Mississippi to the other.

★ **Forks of the Road Slave Market:** One of the South's two largest slave-trading sites during the 1800s stood at this infamous Natchez intersection.

Vicksburg

★ **Vicksburg Battlefield Museum:** Located at the military park, the museum includes a 250-square-foot (23 sq m) diorama complete with 2,300 miniature soldiers. The diorama is a miniature battlefield, depicting exactly how the Union and Confederate forces faced each other during the siege. You'll get an excellent bird's-eye view of the whole thing!

SEE IT HERE!

VICKSBURG NATIONAL MILITARY PARK

Take a driving tour through the park and learn more about the dramatic events that took place during the 47-day siege of Vicksburg, one of the Civil War's most important battles. The park includes miles of reconstructed trenches, a restored gunboat, and 1,325 historic monuments. It was here that during the siege, many of Vicksburg's civilians escaped harm by living underground in nearby caves. They occasionally had milk and bread to eat, but sometimes they had to eat anything they could get—even rats!

Vicksburg National Military Park

COASTAL REGION

THINGS TO DO: Learn about African American history, check out some rockets, and stroll along the shore.

Hattiesburg

★ **Longleaf Trace:** This "Rails to Trails Conservancy Project" was once 41 miles (66 km) of railway and is now a paved nature trail from Hattiesburg to Prentiss. Horse lovers can ride the equestrian path that runs for 23 miles (37 km) along the trace.

★ **1964 Freedom Summer Trail:** Hattiesburg was where much of the civil rights activity took place during 1964's Freedom Summer. This 15-stop driving tour takes you to historic landmarks in Hattiesburg that commemorate the dramatic events of that year.

★ **African American Military History Museum:** African Americans fought in the Civil War on both sides. Since then, many have been honored for their bravery and heroism as part of the U.S. military forces. Here you can see that history traced back in hundreds of photos, artifacts, and unusual displays.

Biloxi

★ **Maritime and Seafood Industry Museum:** Through an array of exhibits on shrimping, oystering, recreational fishing, wetlands, managing marine resources, charter boats, marine blacksmithing, wooden boatbuilding, net making, and numerous historic photographs and objects, this museum interprets the maritime history of the region.

The Gulf Coast near Biloxi

★ **Blessing of the Fleet:** Every spring, shrimping season begins again! The blessing ritual, begun in 1929, starts with an evergreen wreath being dropped into the water in honor of fishers lost at sea. Shrimping is a major industry in Biloxi, and this event is the centerpiece of a citywide celebration that has expanded to include many other events.

Pascagoula

★ **La Pointe Krebs House/Old Spanish Fort Museum:** Built in 1718, this is the oldest building in the Mississippi Valley still standing. The small museum has Indian artifacts, historical displays, and a children's exhibit.

SEE IT HERE!

GULF COAST GATOR RANCH AND TOURS, PASCAGOULA

Get up close and personal with some of the biggest and oldest alligators around—at least in captivity! If you want to feed live alligators, the place to do it is here at the oldest gator ranch in Mississippi. You can also take a walking tour along the ranch's many protected walkways. Or, if you want to get out into the thick of things, you can catch a ride on an airboat for a gator-sighting tour of the swamp.

Black skimmers an the Mississippi Gulf Coast

MINI-BIO

WALTER INGLIS ANDERSON: GULF COAST ARTIST

He led a lonely life and often spent months and years by himself. But during those times alone, Walter Inglis Anderson (1903–1965) produced some amazing watercolors. His paintings are beautiful depictions of the Gulf region. Born in New Orleans, Anderson lived for a time in Ocean Springs and later in Gautier. He spent many years living on Horn Island. The remote island was uninhabited, and he lived with few possessions other than his art supplies. The Walter Anderson Museum of Art opened in Ocean Springs in 1991.

❓ **Want to know more?** See www. walterandersonmuseum.org/

Ocean Springs

★ **Gulf Islands National Seashore Visitors Center:** Island beaches, sparkling waters, bayous, historic forts, and recreational opportunities are plentiful in Gulf Islands National Seashore, the nation's largest seashore!

★ **Walter Anderson Museum of Art:** WAMA is dedicated to the celebration of the works of Walter Inglis Anderson, an American artist whose depictions of the plants, animals, and people of the Gulf Coast have placed him among the top American painters of the 20th century.

Bay St. Louis

★ **John C. Stennis Space Center:** Come and tour the John C. Stennis Space Center, where you can find vast amounts of information on the various NASA space missions and findings. A truly remarkable museum and a fun spot to spend an afternoon.

WRITING PROJECTS

Check out these ideas for creating campaign brochures and researching famous Mississippians. Or learn about the state quarter and design your own.

118

ART PROJECTS

119

Create a great PowerPoint presentation, illustrate the state song, or try your hand at basketry and beadwork.

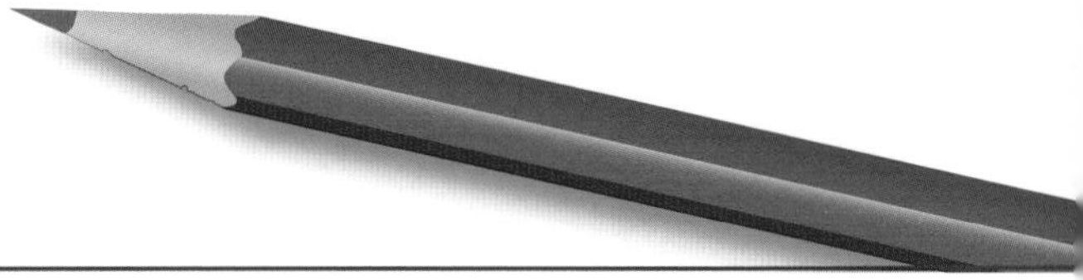

TIMELINE

What happened when? This timeline highlights important events in the state's history—and shows what was happening throughout the United States at the same time.

122

FAST FACTS

Use this section to find fascinating facts about state symbols, land area and population statistics, weather, sports teams, and much more.

126

GLOSSARY

125

Remember the Words to Know from the chapters in this book? They're all collected here.

SCIENCE, TECHNOLOGY, & MATH PROJECTS

Make weather maps, graph population statistics, or research endangered species that live in the state.

120

PRIMARY VS. SECONDARY SOURCES

121

So what are primary and secondary sources? And what's the diff? This section explains all that and where you can find them.

BIOGRAPHICAL DICTIONARY

133

This at-a-glance guide highlights some of the state's most important and influential people. Visit this section to read about their contributions to the state, the country, and the world.

RESOURCES

Books, Web sites, DVDs, and more. Take a look at these additional sources for information about the state.

137

WRITING PROJECTS

★ ★ ★

Create an Election Brochure or Web Site!

Run for office!

Throughout this book, you've read about some of the issues that concern Mississippi today. As a candidate for governor of Mississippi, create a campaign brochure or Web site. Explain how you meet the qualifications to be governor of Mississippi, and talk about the three or four major issues you'll focus on if you're elected. Remember, you'll be responsible for Mississippi's budget. How would you spend the taxpayers' money?

SEE: Chapter Seven, page 87–88.

GO TO: Mississippi's government Web site at www.mississippi.gov.

State Quarter Project

From 1999 to 2008, the U.S. Mint introduced new quarters commemorating each of the 50 states in the order that they were admitted to the Union. Each state's quarter features a unique design on its back, or reverse.

GO TO: www.usmint.gov/kids and find out what's featured on the back of the Mississippi quarter. (Here's a hint: it includes an important plant in the state!)

★ Research the significance of the image. Who designed the quarter? Who chose the final design?

★ Design your own Mississippi state quarter. What images would you choose for the reverse?

★ Make a poster showing the Mississippi quarter and label each image.

Create an interview script with a famous person from Mississippi!

★ Research various famous Mississippians, such as Leontyne Price, Brett Favre, Jim Henson, Fannie Lou Hamer, Faith Hill, James Earl Jones, Walter Payton, or B. B. King, among many others.

★ Based on your research, pick one person you would most like to interview.

★ Write a script of the interview. What questions would you ask? How would this famous person answer? Create a question-and-answer format. You may want to supplement this writing project with a voice-recording dramatization of the interview.

SEE: Chapter Six, pages 75–81 or the Biographical Dictionary on pages 133–136.

GO TO: The Mississippi History Now Web site at http://mshistory.k12.ms.us/index.html to find out more about famous public figures from Mississippi, and their contributions.

ART PROJECTS

★ ★ ★

Create a PowerPoint Presentation or Visitors' Guide

Welcome to Mississippi!

Mississippi's a great place to visit and to live! From its natural beauty to its historical sites, there's plenty to see and do. In your PowerPoint presentation or brochure, highlight 10 to 15 of Mississippi's fascinating landmarks. Be sure to include:

★ a map of the state showing where these sites are located

★ photos, illustrations, Web links, natural history facts, geographic stats, climate and weather, plants and wildlife, and recent discoveries

SEE: Chapter Nine, pages 104–115.

GO TO: The official Web site of Mississippi tourism at www.visitmississippi.org. Download and print maps, photos, national landmark images, and vacation ideas for tourists.

Illustrate the Lyrics to the Mississippi State Song
("Go, Mississippi")

Use markers, paints, photos, collage, colored pencils, or computer graphics to illustrate the lyrics to "Go, Mississippi," the state song. Turn your illustrations into a picture book, or scan them into a PowerPoint and add music!

SEE: The lyrics to "Go, Mississippi" on page 128.

GO TO: The Mississippi state Web site at www. mississippi.gov to find out more about the origin of the Mississippi state song, "Go, Mississippi."

Try Beadwork and Basketry

Like the Native Americans of the Mississippi region, show your creativity by mastering basketry and beadwork. You can make baskets for your own home or as gifts. And you can make jewelry and other beautiful items with beads.

SEE: Chapter Six, pages 74–75.

GO TO: Sites such as www.choctaw.org/culture/ baskets.htm and www.nmai.si.edu/exhibitions/ baskets/subpage.cfm?subpage=tech_tech to learn about the making of baskets, and www.choctaw. org/culture/beadwork.htm for information about beadwork. You can also check your local art associations to see if classes are offered in basket making or beadwork.

Choctaw baskets

SCIENCE, TECHNOLOGY, & MATH PROJECTS

★ ★ ★

Graph Population Statistics!

★ Compare population statistics (such as ethnic background, birth, death, and literacy rates) in Mississippi counties or major cities.

★ On your graph or chart, look at population density, and write sentences describing what the population statistics show; graph one set of population statistics, and write a paragraph explaining what the graphs reveal.

SEE: Chapter Six, pages 68–70.

GO TO: The official Web site for the U.S. Census Bureau at www.census.gov, and at quickfacts.census.gov/qfd/states/28000. html, to find out more about population statistics, how they work, and what the statistics are for Mississippi.

Create a Weather Map of Mississippi!

Use your knowledge of Mississippi's geography to research and identify conditions that result in specific weather events, including thunderstorms and hurricanes. What is it about the geography of Mississippi that makes it vulnerable to things such as hurricanes? Create a weather map or poster that shows the weather patterns over the state. Include a caption, explaining the technology used to measure weather phenomena such as hurricanes.

SEE: Chapter One, pages 15–17.

GO TO: The National Oceanic and Atmospheric Administration's National Weather Service Web site at www.weather.gov for weather maps and forecasts for Mississippi.

Sandhill cranes

Track Endangered Species

Using your knowledge of Mississippi's wildlife, research what animals and plants are endangered or threatened. Find out what the state is doing to protect these species. Chart known populations of the animals and plants, and report on changes in certain geographical areas.

SEE: Chapter One, pages 20–21.

GO TO: Sites such as www.endangeredspecie. com/states/ms.htm

PRIMARY VS. SECONDARY SOURCES

★ ★ ★

What's the Diff?

Your teacher may require at least one or two primary sources and one or two secondary sources for your assignment. So, what's the difference between the two?

★ **Primary sources are original.** You are reading the actual words of someone's diary, journal, letter, autobiography, or interview. Primary sources can also be photographs, maps, prints, cartoons, news/film footage, posters, first-person newspaper articles, drawings, musical scores, and recordings. By the way, when you conduct a survey, interview someone, shoot a video, or take photographs to include in a project, you are creating primary sources!

★ **Secondary sources are what you find in encyclopedias, textbooks, articles, biographies, and almanacs.** These are written by a person or group of people who tell about something that happened to someone else. Secondary sources also recount what another person said or did. This book is an example of a secondary source.

Now that you know what primary sources are—where can you find them?

★ **Your school or local library:** Check the library catalog for collections of original writings, government documents, musical scores, and so on. Some of this material may be stored on microfilm. The Library of Congress Web site (www.loc.gov) is an excellent online resource for primary source materials.

★ **Historical societies:** These organizations keep historical documents, photographs, and other materials. Staff members can help you find what you are looking for. History museums are also great places to see primary sources firsthand.

★ **The Internet:** There are lots of sites that have primary sources you can download and use in a project or assignment.

TIMELINE

★ ★ ★

U.S. Events `1500` **Mississippi Events**

1500s
Choctaw, Chickasaw, and Natchez tribes inhabit what is now Mississippi.

1541
Spanish conquistador Hernando de Soto and his men arrive in what is now Mississippi.

1565
Spanish admiral Pedro Menéndez de Avilés founds St. Augustine, Florida, the oldest continuously occupied European settlement in the continental United States. `1600`

1620
Pilgrims found Plymouth Colony, the second permanent English settlement.

1699
Pierre Le Moyne, Sieur d'Iberville, establishes Fort Maurepas at Old Biloxi.

`1700`

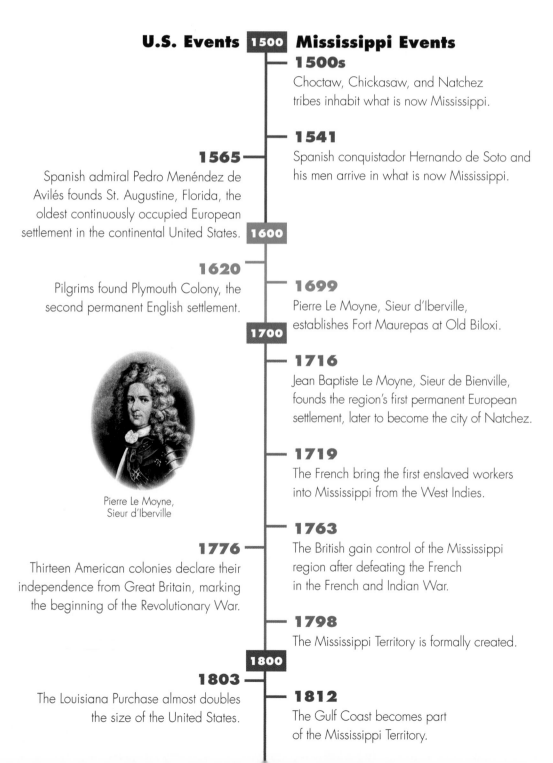

Pierre Le Moyne,
Sieur d'Iberville

1716
Jean Baptiste Le Moyne, Sieur de Bienville, founds the region's first permanent European settlement, later to become the city of Natchez.

1719
The French bring the first enslaved workers into Mississippi from the West Indies.

1763
The British gain control of the Mississippi region after defeating the French in the French and Indian War.

1776
Thirteen American colonies declare their independence from Great Britain, marking the beginning of the Revolutionary War.

1798
The Mississippi Territory is formally created.

`1800`

1803
The Louisiana Purchase almost doubles the size of the United States.

1812
The Gulf Coast becomes part of the Mississippi Territory.

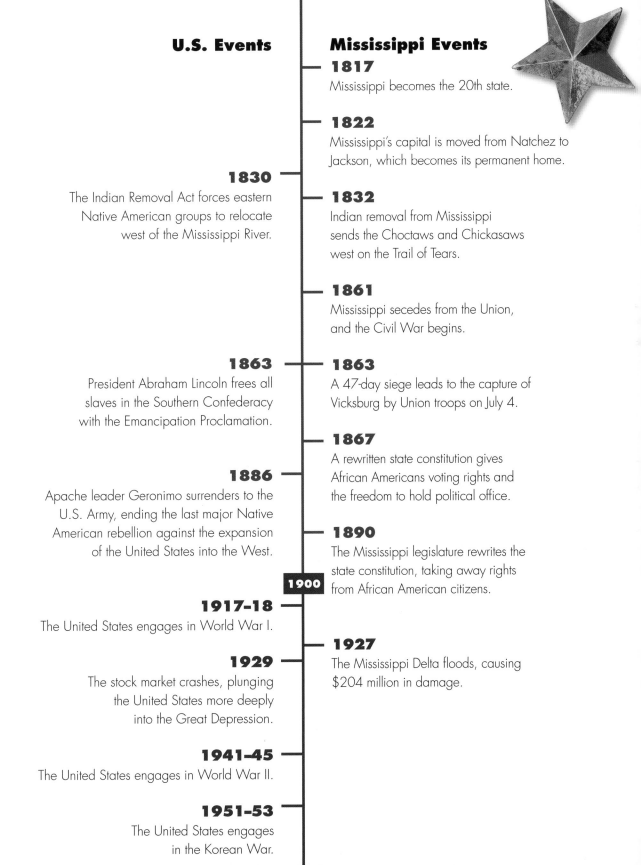

U.S. Events

Mississippi Events

1817
Mississippi becomes the 20th state.

1822
Mississippi's capital is moved from Natchez to Jackson, which becomes its permanent home.

1830
The Indian Removal Act forces eastern Native American groups to relocate west of the Mississippi River.

1832
Indian removal from Mississippi sends the Choctaws and Chickasaws west on the Trail of Tears.

1861
Mississippi secedes from the Union, and the Civil War begins.

1863
President Abraham Lincoln frees all slaves in the Southern Confederacy with the Emancipation Proclamation.

1863
A 47-day siege leads to the capture of Vicksburg by Union troops on July 4.

1867
A rewritten state constitution gives African Americans voting rights and the freedom to hold political office.

1886
Apache leader Geronimo surrenders to the U.S. Army, ending the last major Native American rebellion against the expansion of the United States into the West.

1890
The Mississippi legislature rewrites the state constitution, taking away rights from African American citizens.

1900

1917–18
The United States engages in World War I.

1927
The Mississippi Delta floods, causing $204 million in damage.

1929
The stock market crashes, plunging the United States more deeply into the Great Depression.

1941–45
The United States engages in World War II.

1951–53
The United States engages in the Korean War.

U.S. Events

Mississippi Events

1962
Riots break out and two people are killed when African American James Meredith enrolls at the University of Mississippi.

1963
Medgar Evers, head of the NAACP in Mississippi, is murdered in Jackson.

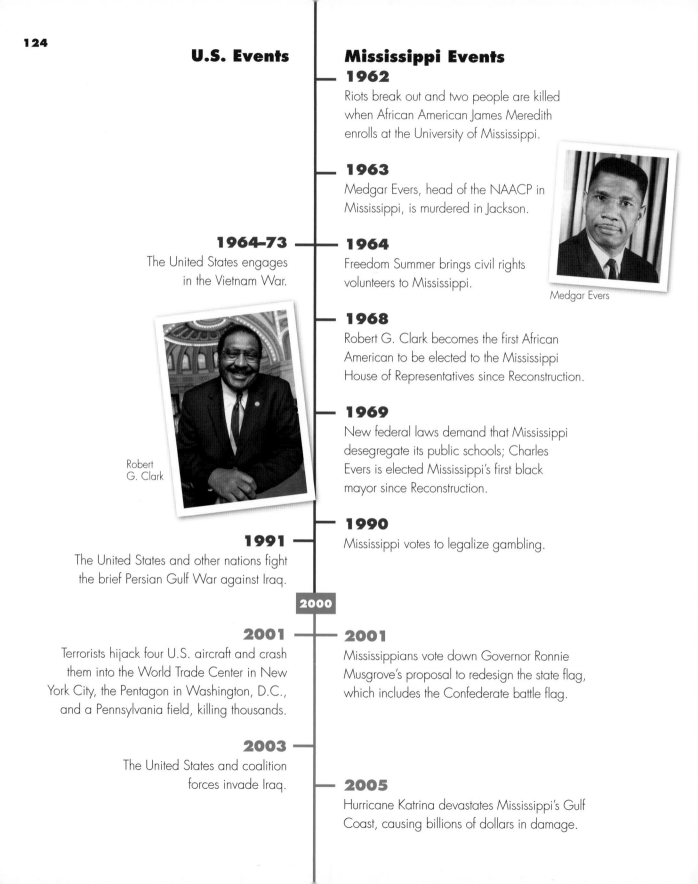

Medgar Evers

1964–73
The United States engages in the Vietnam War.

1964
Freedom Summer brings civil rights volunteers to Mississippi.

1968
Robert G. Clark becomes the first African American to be elected to the Mississippi House of Representatives since Reconstruction.

Robert G. Clark

1969
New federal laws demand that Mississippi desegregate its public schools; Charles Evers is elected Mississippi's first black mayor since Reconstruction.

1990
Mississippi votes to legalize gambling.

1991
The United States and other nations fight the brief Persian Gulf War against Iraq.

2000

2001
Terrorists hijack four U.S. aircraft and crash them into the World Trade Center in New York City, the Pentagon in Washington, D.C., and a Pennsylvania field, killing thousands.

2001
Mississippians vote down Governor Ronnie Musgrove's proposal to redesign the state flag, which includes the Confederate battle flag.

2003
The United States and coalition forces invade Iraq.

2005
Hurricane Katrina devastates Mississippi's Gulf Coast, causing billions of dollars in damage.

GLOSSARY

★ ★ ★

allies people who are on the same side in a conflict

alluvial sand, silt, clay, and gravel that are deposited by running water

bayous streams that run slowly through swamps and lead to or from a river

civil rights the basic rights of every citizen

conquistador one who conquers; specifically a leader in the Spanish conquest of the Americas

discrimination unfair treatment of a person or group

doctrine a principle that is taught, or a system of belief

dysentery a disease marked by severe diarrhea and caused by infection

floodplain land next to a river or stream that experiences periodic flooding

glaciers slow-moving masses of ice

integration the bringing together of all members of society as equals

levees human-made embankments used to prevent flooding

litter a cushioned mat or platform attached to poles for carrying a passenger, sometimes curtained for privacy

malaria a disease marked by chills and fever; it is caused by parasites and spread by mosquito bites

matrilineal relating to tracing a family line through the mother's side

missionary a person who spreads faith and religion to others

mutineers people who defy a leader and rebel against authority to gain power

reforms changes to improve something

savannahs treeless plains

secession the withdrawal from a group or organization

segregation the act of separating people based on race or class

siege a military strategy in which a city or fortress is surrounded, cutting off supplies, and repeatedly attacked until the enemy surrenders

vagrancy the condition of wandering from place to place, lacking a home and money

yeomen people who cultivate a small farm

FAST FACTS

★　★　★

State Symbols

Statehood date	December 10, 1817, the 20th state
Origin of state name	Probably from the Ojibwa words *misi-ziibi*, meaning "great river"
State capital	Jackson
State nickname	Magnolia State
State motto	*Virtute et Armis* ("By Valor and Arms")
State bird	Mockingbird
State flower	Magnolia
State fish	Largemouth bass
State shell	Oyster shell
State insect	Honeybee
State song	"Go, Mississippi" (see lyrics on page 128)
State tree	Magnolia
State waterfowl	Wood duck
State land mammal	White-tailed deer
State water mammal	Bottle-nosed dolphin
State fossil	Prehistoric whale
State stone	Petrified wood
State beverage	Milk
State fair	Jackson (early October)

State seal

Geography

Total area; rank	48,430 square miles (125,434 sq km); 32nd
Land; rank	46,907 square miles (121,489 sq km); 31st
Water; rank	1,523 square miles (3,945 sq km); 24th
Inland water; rank	785 square miles (2,033 sq km); 27th
Coastal water; rank	590 square miles (1,528 sq km); 10th
Territorial water; rank	148 square miles (383 sq km); 19th
Geographic center	Leake County, 9 miles (14 km) northwest of Carthage
Latitude	30° 13' N to 35° N
Longitude	88° 7' W to 91° 41' W
Highest point	Woodall Mountain, 806 feet (246 m)

The mockingbird is the state bird.

Lowest point	Sea level at the Gulf Coast
Largest city	Jackson
Number of counties	82
Longest river	Mississippi River

Population

Population; rank (2006 estimate)	2,910,540; 31st
Density (2006 estimate)	62 persons per square mile (24 per sq km)
Population distribution (2000 census)	49% urban, 51% rural
Ethnic distribution (2005 estimate)	White persons: 61.2%*
	Black persons: 36.9%*
	Asian persons: 0.7%*
	American Indian and Alaska Native persons: 0.4%*
	Native Hawaiian and Other Pacific Islander: 0.0%*
	Persons reporting two or more races: 0.6%
	Persons of Hispanic or Latino origin: 1.7%†
	White persons not Hispanic: 59.7%

† Includes persons reporting only one race.
* Hispanics may be of any race, so they are also included in applicable race categories.

Weather

Record high temperature	115°F (46°C) at Holly Springs on July 29, 1930
Record low temperature	−19°F (−28°C) at Corinth on January 30, 1966
Average July temperature	81°F (27°C)
Average January temperature	45°F (7°C)
Average annual precipitation	56 inches (142 cm)

State flag

STATE SONG

★ ★ ★

"Go, Mississippi"

Interestingly, the Mississippi state song was adopted through the efforts of real estate people. The Jackson Board of Realtors took the initiative and set up an advisory committee for the purpose of finding an appropriate state song. The committee recommended to the state legislature "Go, Mississippi," with words and music by Houston Davis. On May 17, 1962, "Go, Mississippi" was adopted by the legislature as the official song of Mississippi.

Verse:
States may sing their songs of praise
With waving flags and hip-hoo-rays,
Let cymbals crash and let bells ring
'Cause here's one song I'm proud to sing.

Choruses:
Go, Mississippi, keep rolling along,
Go, Mississippi, you cannot go wrong,
Go, Mississippi, we're singing your song,
M-I-S-S-I-S-S-I-P-P-I
Go, Mississippi, you're on the right track,
Go, Mississippi, and this is a fact,
Go, Mississippi, it's your state and mine,
M-I-S-S-I-S-S-I-P-P-I
Go, Mississippi, continue to roll,
Go, Mississippi, the top is the goal,
Go, Mississippi, you'll have and you'll hold,
M-I-S-S-I-S-S-I-P-P-I
Go, Mississippi, get up and go,
Go, Mississippi, let the world know,
That our Mississippi is leading the show,
M-I-S-S-I-S-S-I-P-P-I

NATURAL AREAS AND HISTORIC SITES

★ ★ ★

National Battlefield Sites and Military Parks

Brices Cross Roads National Battlefield Site preserves the setting of a Civil War battle.

Tupelo National Battlefield is the site of a Civil War engagement in 1864.

Vicksburg National Military Park is the site of a 47-day siege that ended in the surrender of the city to Union forces.

National Historical Park

Natchez National Historical Park contains preserved buildings from before the Civil War.

National Seashore

Gulf Islands National Seashore covers 135,625 acres (54,885 ha) along the Gulf Coast.

National Scenic Trail

The *Natchez Trace National Scenic Trail* follows part of the 444-mile (715 km) Natchez Trace Parkway.

National Parkway

The *Natchez Trace Parkway* follows the historic route of Native Americans and early settlers from Mississippi to Tennessee.

State Parks

Mississippi had 28 state park units in 2006.

SPORTS TEAMS

★ ★ ★

NCAA Teams (Division I)

Alcorn State University *Braves*
Jackson State University *Tigers*
Mississippi State University *Bulldogs*
Mississippi Valley State University *Delta Devils*
University of Mississippi *Rebels*
University of Southern Mississippi *Golden Eagles*

Fans celebrate an Ole Miss basketball victory.

CULTURAL INSTITUTIONS

★ ★ ★

Libraries

The *Mississippi State Library* (Jackson) is the oldest library in the state.

The *University of Mississippi, Mississippi State University,* and the *University of Southern Mississippi* all have academic libraries.

Museums

The *Mississippi Museum of Art* (Jackson), the state's largest art museum, emphasizes American art.

The *Meridian Museum of Art* (Meridian) features works of Mississippi artists and promotes art education throughout the community.

The *Delta Blues Museum* (Clarksdale) includes videotaped presentations, photographs, sound-and-slide shows, and memorabilia of blues artists and their music.

Smith Robertson Museum and Cultural Center (Jackson) has exhibits that depict the experience and heritage of black Mississippians from their African roots to the present.

Performing Arts

Mississippi has one major symphony orchestra, two ballet companies, and two opera companies.

Universities and Colleges

In 2006, Mississippi had 25 public and 13 private institutions of higher learning.

ANNUAL EVENTS

January–March

Dixie National Livestock Show and Rodeo in Jackson (February)

Mardi Gras festivities in various cities on the Mississippi Gulf Coast and in Natchez (February)

Garden Club Pilgrimages of pre-Civil War homes in Aberdeen, Columbus, Holly Springs, Natchez, Port Gibson, Vicksburg, and other communities (March–April)

April–June

D'Iberville Landing and Historical Ball in Ocean Springs (April)

Natchez Trace Festival in Kosciusko (April)

Railroad Festival in Amory (April)

World Catfish Festival in Belzoni (April)

Atwood Bluegrass Festival in Monticello (May)

Blessing of the Fleet and Shrimp Festival in Biloxi (May)

Jubilee Jam Art and Music Festival in Jackson (May)

Flea Market in Canton (May)

Jimmie Rodgers Memorial Festival in Meridian (May)

Civil War Reenactment in Vicksburg (May)

Mississippi International Balloon Classic in Greenwood (June)

July–September

Choctaw Indian Fair in Philadelphia (July)

Mississippi Deep Sea Fishing Rodeo in Gulfport (July)

Watermelon Festival in Mize (July)

Crop Day in Greenwood (August)

Neshoba County Fair in Philadelphia (August)

Delta Blues Festival in Greenville (September)

Seafood Festival in Jackson (September)

October–December

Flea Market in Canton (October)

Mississippi State Fair in Jackson (second week of October)

Natchez Fall Pilgrimage in Natchez (October)

Scottish Highland Games in Biloxi (November)

Christmas in Natchez (December)

Trees of Christmas Festival in Meridian (December)

Walter Inglis Anderson See page 115.

A-push-ma-ta-ha-hu-bi See page 30.

Ross Barnett (1898–1987) was the governor of Mississippi during the volatile civil rights era. As governor, he defied the law in an attempt to keep the University of Mississippi segregated.

Blanche K. Bruce See page 90.

Robert G. Clark See page 89.

Jefferson Davis See page 51.

Hernando de Soto (1496–1542) was the first known European to come upon the Mississippi River. He was a Spanish conquistador who explored the Mississippi Delta region and engaged in skirmishes with the Native Americans.

Charles Evers (1922–) was a civil rights activist, politician, and brother of civil rights activist Medgar Evers. Charles was an early field director of the National Association for the Advancement of Colored People. He became the South's first African American mayor in 1969.

Charles Evers

Medgar Evers See page 63.

William Faulkner (1897–1962) wrote award-winning short fiction and novels based on his experiences as a Mississippian. He won the Nobel Prize for Literature in 1949.

Brett Favre (1969–) is the National Football League's starting quarterback for the Green Bay Packers, with whom he has played since 1992. Part French and part Choctaw, he is the only player to be named the NFL's Most Valuable Player three times. He led his team to victory in the 1997 Super Bowl. Favre was born in Gulfport.

Brett Favre

Morgan Freeman (1937–) was born in Memphis, Tennessee, and makes his home in Charleston. He is an Academy Award-winning actor, as well as a film director and narrator.

Evelyn Gandy See page 88.

Robert Gleed (1836–1916) was an escaped slave who settled in Columbus. A landowner and businessman, he served in the state senate for two terms.

Elizabeth Taylor Greenfield (1809–1876) was a famed African American opera singer, nicknamed the Black Swan. Born in Natchez, Greenfield grew up and spent most of her life in Philadelphia, Pennsylvania. She performed for white audiences in the United States, Canada, and Europe. She was the first and, during her lifetime, the only black opera star in America.

John Grisham (1955–) is a former politician, a retired attorney, and an international best-selling novelist. He is a strong supporter of continuing the southern literary tradition. He has endowed scholarships and writers' residencies at the University of Mississippi to support southern writers.

Fannie Lou Hamer See page 64.

James D. Hardy (1918–2003) was a renowned physician who, in 1963, performed the world's first transplant of a human lung into another human being. The next year, he performed the controversial operation of transplanting a chimpanzee heart into a human body, with only brief success. Two of many books authored by Hardy became standard textbooks for doctors studying surgery.

Jim Henson See page 75.

Faith Hill (1967–) is an award-winning country music artist, who is extremely proud of her Mississippi roots. She was born in Jackson.

David Holmes See page 86.

James Earl Jones

James Earl Jones (1931–) is a stage and film actor who was born in Arkabutla. His ancestry includes African American, Irish, and Cherokee Indian. After graduating from college in Michigan and serving in the military, he began to get film roles. One of his best-known credits is as the voice of Darth Vader in the Star Wars movies.

B. B. King See page 78.

John Roy Lynch (1847–1939) was Mississippi's first African American speaker of the house. Raised in slavery, he became the first African American voted into public office in Mississippi. He served as a congressman and was the author of *The Facts of Reconstruction*, an important text that is still widely consulted.

Phillip Martin See page 101.

James Meredith See page 62.

McKinley "Muddy Waters" Morganfield (1915–1983) was a world-famous blues musician who played guitar and harmonica. He was born in Rolling Fork, in the Mississippi Delta, and got his nickname from his grandmother.

Faith Hill

Willie Morris (1934–1999) was an author who was born in Jackson and grew up in Yazoo City. He served as editor in chief of *Harper's* magazine and wrote *My Dog Skip*.

Mussacunna See page 28.

Brandy Rayana Norwood (1979–) is an actress and Grammy-winning pop singer. Professionally known simply as Brandy, she began her career in her teens, first in TV commercials and then starring in the hit sitcom *Moesha*. She has sold millions of albums worldwide and was nominated for a dozen Grammy awards between 1996 and 2005.

Walter Payton (1954–1999) was a running back for the Chicago Bears. Payton, a Pro Football Hall of Fame member, distinguished himself as one of the National Football League's most productive and memorable players. He set many rushing records during his professional and collegiate careers. He was born in Columbia.

Robert Pittman (1953–) created the world-renowned cable TV station MTV, which features music videos, interviews with celebrities, and other entertainment content. Pittman was born in Jackson.

Elvis Presley

Elvis Presley (1935–1977) was known as the King of Rock 'n' Roll. He was born in Tupelo and became a worldwide music idol. Besides having many hit records, he starred in numerous feature films.

Leontyne Price (1927–) rose from poverty to become one of the greatest opera sopranos of all time. She is acclaimed especially for her performances in *Aida*.

Quigaltam (ca. 1500s) was Great Sun, or chief, of the Natchez Indians. Quigaltam drove de Soto's men down the Mississippi River and away from North America.

Hiram Revels (1822–1901) was the first African American to serve in the U.S. Senate. Born in Fayetteville, North Carolina, he became a minister and moved to Natchez in 1866. After being elected to the state senate in 1869, he was elected to serve out the remainder of Jefferson Davis's term in the U.S. Senate. He held that office from 1870 to 1871.

Walter Payton

Jerry Rice See page 81.

LeAnn Rimes (1982–) is a country music singer. Jackson-born Rimes recorded her first album at age 11. At 14, she became the youngest person ever to win a Grammy Award when she won for Best Female Country Vocal Performance, as well as for Best New Artist. Her crossover hit, "How Do I Live," remained on the Billboard Hot 100 music charts for a record-breaking 69 weeks.

John Cornelius Stennis (1901–1995) was a U.S. senator from Mississippi. He spent 60 years as a politician, most of those years as a senator. He was renowned for his high ethical standards and his dedication to serving the people.

Jacob M. Valentine See page 21.

Eudora Welty See page 76.

Tennessee Williams

Thomas Lanier "Tennessee" Williams (1911–1983) was a Pulitzer Prize–winning playwright. He was born in Columbus but grew up in St. Louis, Missouri. He got his nickname from college classmates who weren't sure which southern state he was from. Williams wrote numerous plays, some of which were adapted as movies. He won Pulitzers for *A Streetcar Named Desire* and *Cat on a Hot Tin Roof*, both of which are now considered classics.

Oprah Winfrey (1954–) is an actress and host of the long-running *Oprah Winfrey Show* on television. She also publishes the magazine *O*. She was born in poverty in Kosciusko but is now one of the wealthiest women in the world.

William Winter (1923–) was governor of Mississippi from 1980 to 1984. He is known for his strong support of public education, racial reconciliation, and historic preservation.

Richard Wright See page 77.

Oprah Winfrey

RESOURCES

BOOKS

Nonfiction

Deady, Kathleen W. *Mississippi* (Land of Liberty). Mankato, Minn.: Capstone Press, 2003.

Fireside, Harvey. *The Mississippi Burning Civil Rights Murder Conspiracy: A Headline Court Case*. Berkeley Heights, N.J.: Enslow Publishers, 2002.

Gaines, Ann. *Faith Hill* (Real-Life Reader Biographies). Hockessin, Del.: Mitchell Lane Publishers, 2001.

Ishizuka, Kathy. *John Grisham: Best-Selling Author* (People to Know). Berkeley Heights, N.J.: Enslow Publishers, 2003.

Litwin, Laura Baskes. *Fannie Lou Hamer: Fighting for the Right to Vote* (African-American Biographies). Berkeley Heights, N.J.: Enslow Publishers, 2002.

Moore, Heidi. *Medgar Evers* (American Lives). Chicago: Heinemann Library, 2005.

Stewart, Mark. *Jerry Rice* (Grolier All-Pro Biographies). Danbury, Conn.: Children's Press, 1998.

Towle, Mike. *Walter Payton: Football's "Sweetest" Superstar* (Great American Sports Legends). Nashville: Cumberland House Publishing, 2005.

Fiction

Holling, Holling C. *Minn of the Mississippi*. New York: Houghton Mifflin, 1978.

McMullan, Margaret. *How I Found the Strong*. New York: Laurel Leaf, 2006.

Naylor, Phyllis Reynolds. *Night Cry*. New York: Atheneum, 1984.

Taylor, Mildred D. *Let the Circle Be Unbroken*. New York: Puffin Classics, reissue 1991.

Taylor, Mildred D. *Roll of Thunder, Hear My Cry*. New York: Puffin Classics, reissue 1991.

DVDs

B.B. King: Live by Request. MCA, 2003.
Brett Favre: On and Off the Field. Triumph Marketing, 2004.
Discoveries . . . America: Mississippi. Bennett-Watt Entertainment, 2005.
Mississippi State Secrets. A&E Home Video, 2006.
Odyssey: Myths and Moundbuilders. PBS Video, 1981.

WEB SITES AND ORGANIZATIONS

B. B. King Museum

www.bbkingmuseum.org
Learn about the new museum dedicated to
blues great B. B. King.

Mississippi Band of Choctaw Indians

www.choctaw.org
Explore many aspects of the Mississippi
Choctaw Native American culture.

Mississippi Government

www.mississippi.gov
Learn about the current news and happenings
in Mississippi, as well as details and facts
about the state government.

Mississippi History Now

http://mshistory.k12.ms.us/index.html
Find out about practically any aspect of
Mississippi history at Mississippi History
Now, the online publication of the Mississippi
Historical Society.

Mississippi Library Commission

http://www.mlc.lib.ms.us/
ServicesToGeneralPublic/MississippiTrivia.htm
Start your discovery of Mississippi at the
Mississippi Library Commission's trivia page.
It's full of interesting facts.

Visit Mississippi

http://visitmississippi.org/
cultural%5Fhistorical/
Get the detailed where-and-when facts about
Mississippi's many historical and cultural
landmarks right here, as well as information
about fascinating attractions to visit and
things to do.

INDEX

★ ★ ★

AUTHOR'S TIPS AND SOURCE NOTES

★ ★ ★

For me, researching and writing a book about Mississippi began as quite a challenge.

To understand the state's turbulent history, I read a fascinating book by John Ray Skates titled *Mississippi: A Bicentennial History*. This book provided a deeply thoughtful interpretation of how and why racism evolved in Mississippi. Reading it gave me the opportunity to understand the dramatic historical events and the varied human personalities that shaped Mississippi's image and attitudes over time.

I got many further insights by reading *Mississippi: An American Journey*, by Anthony Walton. This autobiographical account expanded and enriched my awareness of Mississippi's complex past, present, and personality. Walton's book records a trip he took, as a well-educated African American from the North, to his parents' home state.

The Internet provided innumerable sites full of material on every aspect of Mississippi. I also had many phone conversations with helpful people all over the state. These included, especially, Betty McLin and Savannah Kelly at the Eudora Welty Public Library in Jackson; and T. K. Saul, historian at the Old Court House Museum in Vicksburg. In the end, I discovered Mississippi to be a state of great beauty, hospitality, culture, humor, and surprising richness.